CW01497696

Daily
Moments

Pause to Reflect

Daily Moments

Pause to Reflect

Written and compiled by Abi May

Published by Abi May

2016

First Printing: 2016

ISBN 978-1-326-76427-2

Published by Abi May
Staffordshire, England

www.abi.mayihelp.co.uk

Acknowledgements

Unless otherwise indicated, all scriptures are in the New International Version (NIV UK) or New King James Version (NKJV).

NIVUK: Holy Bible, New International Version® Anglicized, NIV® Copyright © 1979, 1984, 2011 by Biblica, Inc.® Used by permission. All rights reserved worldwide.

New King James Version: Copyright © 1982 by Thomas Nelson, Inc. Used by permission. All rights reserved.

Scriptures indicated as *WEB* are from the *World English Bible*.

Scriptures indicated as *KJV* are from the *King James Version*, also known as the Authorized Version, 1611.

Scriptures indicated as *NLT* are from the New Living Translation, copyright © 1996, 2004, 2015 by Tyndale House Foundation. Used by permission of Tyndale House Publishers Inc., Carol Stream, Illinois 60188. All rights reserved.

Every effort has been made to authenticate the origin of quotations and obtain the permission of authors where quotations are not in the public domain. The editor offers her apologies for any unintentional oversights and asks that you notify the publishers in order for corrections to be made in subsequent editions.

All texts without attribution are original and © copyright Abi May 2016.

Notes

Daily Moments is a book of short daily readings compiled from a variety of historical and contemporary sources, along with original texts by the author.

Due to the range of authors, times and languages, you will find a variety of styles, with differing conventions for punctuation, capitalisation, spelling and grammar. Some older quotations have been adapted into more modern language for easier reading. British/American spellings, capitalisation, and other grammatical and typographical differences have also been standardised in some cases.

In memory of Pax and Catherine

Introduction

It can just take a few words to change the tone of your day, lifting you above the daily grind. Some well-placed words can cheer you up; motivate you to keep going; inspire you with a new perspective on a familiar topic.

These daily readings don't have many words. Each page can be easily read in ten, five or even two minutes. Quotations, poetry extracts, short readings and scriptures have been carefully selected to provide the maximum impact for the minimum of words.

To get the most from this book, I invite you to take yourself to a quiet place—environmentally and inwardly quiet if possible—so that you can focus on what you read. Reflect upon the message on the day's page. Does it ring true for you? How does it apply?

You may like to turn your thoughts into prayers, and perhaps write notes or additional scriptures that come to mind.

Instead of the day's page, you may sometimes want to choose a topic from the index at the back of the book.

Reflective reading brings its own rewards. I hope it also brings you a sense of closeness to the lasting source of inspiration, Jesus, our Lord.

Abi May

**Hope smiles from the threshold
of the year to come,
Whispering 'it will be happier.'**

Alfred Tennyson

And now let us believe in a long year that is given to us, new, untouched, full of things that have never been.

Rainer Maria Rilke

The New Year comes to us with smiles, because it comes rich and beautiful with the boundless treasures of hope. We know not what the New Year may have in store for us, of good or of evil, but still we greet it hopefully, because we trust in the loving-kindness of our God. He will mix our cup for us, and his hand is that of a loving Father.

In our anticipations of what is to come, hope predominates and hope has its roots in the boundless goodness of God.

Arthur Charles Hervey

"For I know the plans I have for you," says the Lord. "They are plans for good and not for disaster, to give you a future and a hope."

Jeremiah 29:11 (NLT)

I am the new year.

I am an unspoiled page in your book of time. I am your next chance at the art of living. I am your opportunity to practice what you have learned about life during the last twelve months.

All that you sought and didn't find is hidden in me, waiting for you to search it but with more determination. All the good that you tried for and didn't achieve is mine to grant when you have fewer conflicting desires.

All that you dreamed but didn't dare to do, all that you hoped but did not will, all the faith that you claimed but did not have—these slumber lightly, waiting to be awakened by the touch of a strong purpose.

I am your opportunity to renew your allegiance to Him who said, "Behold, I make all things new."[1]

Author unknown. [1]Revelation 21:5

For last year's words belong to
last year's language
And next year's words await another voice.

T. S. Eliot

Therefore, if anyone is in Christ, he is a new creation; old things have passed away; behold, all things have become new.

2 Corinthians 5:17

He has redeemed my soul in peace.

Psalm 55:18

For He Himself is our peace.

Ephesians 2:14

All the peace and favour of the world cannot calm a troubled heart; but where this peace is which Christ gives, all the trouble and disquiet of the world cannot disturb it.

Robert Leighton

Submarine navigators tell us from their experience that storms do not reach very deep into the ocean. The water is perfectly calm a hundred feet down, no matter how high the breakers may rise on the surface. There is quiet in the depths that no surface storms can disturb. This is possible, too, in human lives; there can be serenity and peace within, undisturbed by the storms of the world. Jesus is our peace.

Author unknown

Now acquaint yourself with Him,
and be at peace;
Thereby good will come to you.

Job 22:21

Then you shall go on forward from there.

1 Samuel 10:3

God never puts any man in a space too small to grow in.

Author unknown

Nothing ever built arose to touch the skies unless some man dreamed that it should, some man believed that it could, and some man willed that it must.

Charles F. Kettering

I find the great thing in this world is not so much where we stand, as in what direction we are moving.

Oliver Wendell Holmes

In activity we must find our joy as well as glory; and labour, like everything else that is good, is its own reward.

Edwin Percy Whipple

Far away there in the sunshine are my highest aspirations. I may not reach them but I can look up and see their beauty, believe in them and try to follow where they lead.

Louisa May Alcott

You will make your prayer to Him, He will hear you.

Job 22:27

Certain thoughts are prayers. There are moments when, whatever be the attitude of the body, the soul is on its knees.

Victor Hugo

How God works in answer to prayer is a mystery that logic cannot penetrate, but that He does work in answer to prayer is gloriously true.

Oswald Chambers

Some prayers have a longer voyage than others, but they return with the richer cargo at last, so that the praying soul is a gainer by waiting for an answer.

William Gurnall

Jesus said to her, "Did I not say to you that if you would believe you would see the glory of God?" Therefore I say to you, whatever things you ask when you pray, believe that you receive them, and you will have them.

John 11:40; Mark 11:24

The visit of the Three Wise Men

Now after Jesus was born in Bethlehem of Judea in the days of Herod the king, behold, wise men from the East came to Jerusalem, saying, "Where is He who has been born King of the Jews? For we have seen His star in the East and have come to worship Him."

The star which they had seen in the East went before them, till it came and stood over where the young Child was. When they saw the star, they rejoiced with exceedingly great joy. And when they had come into the house, they saw the young Child with Mary His mother, and fell down and worshipped Him. And when they had opened their treasures, they presented gifts to Him: gold, frankincense, and myrrh.

Matthew 2:1–2, 9–11

What can I give Him
As small as I am?
If I were a shepherd
I'd give Him a lamb.
If I were a wise man
I'd do my part.
I know what I'll give Him,
I'll give Him my heart.

Christina Rossetti

The path of the just is like the shining sun, that shines ever brighter unto the perfect day.

Proverbs 4:18

Watch your way then, as a cautious traveller; and don't be gazing at that mountain or river in the distance, and saying, 'How shall I ever get over them?' but keep to the present *little inch* that is before you, and accomplish *that* in the little moment that belongs to it. The mountain and the river can only be passed in the same way; and, when you come to them, you will come to the light and strength that belong to them.

M. A. Kelty

Wherever He may guide me,
  No want shall turn me back;
My Shepherd is beside me,
  And nothing can I lack.
His wisdom ever waketh,
  His sight is never dim,
He knows the way He taketh,
  And I will walk with Him.

Anna Laetitia Waring

I'll bless you every day,
and keep it up from now to eternity.

Psalm 145:2 MSG

My voice You shall hear in the morning, O LORD; In the morning I will direct it to You, And I will look up.

Psalm 5:3

O Lord,

Grant me the blessing of greeting the coming day in peace. Help me in all things to rely upon your holy will. In every hour of the day reveal your will to me. Bless my dealings with all who surround me.

Teach me to treat all that comes to me throughout the day with peace of soul and with firm conviction that your will governs us all. In all my deeds and words guide my thoughts and feelings. In unforeseen events let me not forget that all are sent by you.

Teach me to act firmly and wisely, without embittering and embarrassing others. Give me strength to bear the fatigue of this coming day with all that it shall bring.

Direct my will, teach me to pray, pray yourself in me.

Filaret Drozdov, adapted

Think about the good things.

Philippians 4:8, paraphrased

An unhappy woman, dissatisfied with her lot in life, was struck by an account of a would-be emigrant who sold everything he had on an internet auction site, including his house and all of its contents, his car, and even an invitation to meet his friends. Starting again sounded a good prospect, so she decided to follow suit.

She wrote a detailed advertisement, describing her flat and possessions, her circle of friends, and the nice places to visit in her neighbourhood.

"How does this sound?" she asked herself, hoping her advert would invite generous bids. As she read the draft aloud, it suddenly struck her that if she had seen an advertisement like this five years earlier, she would have jumped at the chance to have everything that this person described. But she already had it!

Her advertisement was never posted.

As Bob Gass has wisely written, "Contentment isn't getting what we want, but enjoying what we've got."

Retold

To have found God is not an end in itself but a beginning.

Franz Rosenzweig

Out of heaven He let you hear His voice, that He might instruct you.

Deuteronomy 4:36

We need never shout across the spaces to an absent God. He is nearer than our own soul, closer than our most secret thoughts.

Aiden Wilson Tozer

It is in silence that God is known, and through mysteries that he declares himself.

Robert Hugh Benson

Seek in reading and you will find in meditation; knock in prayer and it shall be opened to you in contemplation.

St. John of the Cross

We need to find God, and He cannot be found in noise and restlessness. See how nature, the trees, the flowers and the grass grow in perfect silence. ... We need to be alone with God in silence to be renewed and to be transformed. For silence can give us a new outlook on life. In it we are filled with the grace of God, which makes us do all things with joy.

Mother Teresa

He has filled them with skill
to do all manner of work.

Exodus 35:35

All the performances of human art, at which we look with praise or wonder, are instances of the resistless force of perseverance: it is by this that the quarry becomes a pyramid, and that distant countries are united with canals.

If a man was to compare the effect of a single stroke of the pickaxe, or of one impression of the spade, with the general design and last result, he would be overwhelmed by the sense of their disproportion; yet those petty operations, incessantly continued, in time surmount the greatest difficulties, and mountains are levelled, and oceans bounded, by the slender force of human beings.

Samuel Johnson

If you wish success in life, make perseverance your bosom friend, experience your wise counsellor, caution your elder brother, and hope your guardian genius.

Joseph Addison

That I may not thirst

[Jesus] came to a city of Samaria which is called Sychar. ... Now Jacob's well was there. Jesus therefore, being wearied from His journey, sat thus by the well. It was about the sixth hour.

A woman of Samaria came to draw water. Jesus said to her, "Give Me a drink. ... If you knew the gift of God, and who it is who says to you, 'Give Me a drink,' you would have asked Him, and He would have given you living water."

The woman said to Him, "Sir, You have nothing to draw with, and the well is deep. Where then do You get that living water?"

Jesus answered and said to her, "Whoever drinks of this water will thirst again, but whoever drinks of the water that I shall give him will never thirst. But the water that I shall give him will become in him a fountain of water springing up into everlasting life."

The woman said to Him, "Sir, give me this water, that I may not thirst."

John 4:5–15

**Truly the light is sweet,
And a pleasant thing it is for the eyes
to behold the sun.**

Ecclesiastes 11:7

And lo! In a flash of crimson splendour, with blazing, scarlet clouds running before his chariot and heralding his majestic approach, God's sun rises upon the world.

William Makepeace Thackeray

The sun does not shine for a few trees and flowers, but for the wide world's joy. So God sits ... in heaven, not for a favoured few, but for the universe of life.

Henry Ward Beecher

O God of love,
true light and radiance of our world,
shine into our hearts like the rising sun,
and banish the darkness of sin
and the mists of error.
May we, this day and all our life,
walk without stumbling
along the way which you have set
before us;
through your Son Jesus Christ our Lord.

Desiderius Erasmus

My song shall be of you, Lord,
Your mercy crowns my days.
You fill my cup with blessings,
And tune my heart to praise.

Author unknown

Contentment is one of the flowers of heaven, and if we would have it, it must be cultivated. ... Paul says, `I have learned to be content;'[1] as much as to say he did not know how at one time. It cost him some pains to attain to the mystery of that great truth.

Charles Haddon Spurgeon. [1]Phillipians 4:11

Dear Lord,

You have made everything beautiful in its time.[1] Give me joy in my heart to live in this moment, thanking You for Your provision, not only of material necessities, but also of the love and faith that You offer to all those who reach out to You.

Help me to know the reality of your promise, "My grace is sufficient for you."[2] Be My centre and My focus, so that my heart will be at peace.

[1]Ecclesiastes 3:11 [2]2 Corinthians 12:9

**Little deeds of kindness,
little words of love,
Make our earth an Eden
like the heaven above.**

Frances Sargent Osgood

Imagine ... you come upon an old friend dressed in rags and half-starved and say, "Good morning, friend! Be clothed in Christ! Be filled with the Holy Spirit!" and walk off without providing so much as a coat or a cup of soup—where does that get you?

James 2:15–16 MSG

Live for something. Do good and leave behind you a monument of virtue that the storms of time can never destroy. Write your name in kindness, love and mercy on the hearts of thousands you come in contact with, year by year, and you will never be forgotten. Your name and your good deeds will shine as the stars of heaven.

Dr Thomas Chalmers

The eternal God

Oh, the depth of the riches both of the wisdom and knowledge of God! How unsearchable are His judgments and His ways past finding out!

Romans 11:33

As well might a gnat seek to drink in the ocean, as a finite creature to comprehend the Eternal God. A God whom we could understand would be no God. If we could grasp him, he could not be infinite: if we could understand him, then were he not divine.

Charles Haddon Spurgeon

To believe in God for me is to feel that there is a God, not a dead one, or a stuffed one, but a living one, who with irresistible force urges us towards more loving.

Vincent van Gogh

LORD God of Israel, there is no God in heaven above or on earth below like You, who keep Your covenant and mercy with Your servants who walk before You with all their hearts.

1 Kings 8:23

A righteous man regards the life of his animal.

Proverbs 12:10

Then God said, "Let the earth bring forth the living creature according to its kind: cattle and creeping thing and beast of the earth, each according to its kind"; and it was so.

Genesis 1:24

God our heavenly Father, you created the world to serve humanity's needs and to lead them to you. By our own fault we have lost the beautiful relationship which we once had with all your creation. Help us to see that by restoring our relationship with you we will also restore it with all your creation. Give us the grace to see animals as gifts from you and to treat them with respect, for they are your creation. Amen.

Attributed to Francis of Assisi

A day at a time

A family had a few apple trees at the bottom of their garden. The trees yielded more fruit than could be eaten immediately or given to neighbours, so some needed to be stored for the coming months.

One autumn, little Tommy was finally big enough to help his mother store the apples. They had been picked and piled up in a basket with care, as bruised apples will spoil. Now it was time to transfer them to storage racks in the cellar.

Tommy, eager to help, put his arms around a dozen shiny apples and tried to carry them over to the rack. To his dismay, one by one the apples dropped out of his arms until they were all on the floor.

His mother wasn't too worried. "Here, let me show you," she said gently as she put his hands around one apple. "Take this one and put it over there, and then come back and get another one."

Too often we try to put our arms around a year or a month or a week, but God tells us, "Take it a day at a time."[1] We aren't equipped to carry all of our future cares at once, but we can face each challenge as it comes.

Retold. [1]*Matthew 6:34*

Whatever things you ask in prayer, believing, you will receive.

Matthew 21:22

Pray to God at the beginning of all thy works, that so thou mayest bring them all to a good ending.

Xenophon

Prayer touches the only spring that can ensure success. By speaking, we move man; but by prayer, we move God.

Robert Hall

God does not stand afar off as I struggle to speak. He cares enough to listen with more than casual attention. He translates my scrubby words and hears what is truly inside. He hears my sighs and uncertain gropings as fine prose.

Timothy Jones

Talk to him in prayer of all your wants, your troubles, even of the weariness you feel in serving him. You cannot speak too freely, too trustfully, of him.

François de la Mothe-Fénelon

Ask, and you will receive, that your joy may be full.

John 16:24

Be still, and know that I am God.

Psalm 46:10

We may be richer in faith, and so richer in hope, and so richer in joy today, by remembering the certainty of God's gracious promises, and how his word endures to all generations. In quiet hours, when we are laid aside, we may remember, too, that though the world is still the same world—full of disappointments—full of care—full of change—full of uncertainty—yet this one great certainty makes up to the Christian for all else. Truly all things are ours—life, death, things present, things to come, for we are his who says, "I am the Lord, I change not."[1]

Our Father is unchangeable in truth and love; and as we feel afresh our spiritual union with Christ, let us call to mind the words of his apostle John, "We are in him that is true."[2]

William M. Statham. [1]*Malachi 3:6;* [2]*1 John 5:20*

Can we not learn, like tired children, to fall into the everlasting arms and rest, not in what we know, but in whom we trust?

Charles Haddon Spurgeon

Restore to me the joy of Your salvation.

Psalm 51:12

Lord, as the morning sun dawning,
Chase all my darkness away,
And with Thy kind wings of healing
Turn all my night into day.
Come Thou, O come, Lord of comfort,
Come to my sad, weary heart,
Come, O Thou blest hope of glory,
Never, O never depart.

If in the test of my trouble,
Faint be my spirit and heart,
Faith, with the star of hope glimm'ring,
Shall all be taken apart,
May then Thy faith with Thy life-pow'r
Over me hold its full sway
That all Thy riches of glory
Now I may share and for aye.

Lord of all hope,
O how sweet is Thy voice,
Making my heart in Thy presence rejoice.

Witness Lee

Help me, Lord, to lay down my worries and
fears, my struggles with my own inadequacies,
and lean wholly upon You. Shine your light to
banish the darkness. May I rest securely in your
love.

In every country the sun rises in the morning.

Traditional proverb

Not that I have already attained, or am already perfected; but I press on ... reaching forward to those things which are ahead.

Philippians 3:12–13

Every year of my life I grow more convinced that it is wisest and best to fix our attention on the beautiful and the good, and dwell as little as possible on the evil and the false.

Richard Cecil

Faith that increaseth, walking in light;
Hope that aboundeth, glowing and bright;
Love that is perfect, casting out fear,
Crown with rejoicing thine opening year!

Frances Ridley Havergal

The LORD will open to you His good treasure, the heavens, to give the rain to your land in its season, and to bless all the work of your hand.

Deuteronomy 28:12

The greatest use of life is to spend it for something that outlasts it.

William James

God's love, though, is ever and always, eternally present to all who fear him,

Making everything right for them and their children.

Psalm 103:17 MSG

The great danger facing all of us...is not that we shall make an absolute failure of life, nor that we shall fall into outright viciousness, nor that we shall be terribly unhappy, nor that we shall feel [that] life has no meaning at all – not these things.

The danger is that we may fail to perceive life's greatest meaning, fall short of its highest good, miss its deepest and most abiding happiness, be unable to tender the most needed service, be unconscious of life ablaze with the light of the Presence of God - and be content to have it so.

That is the danger: that someday we may wake up and find that always we have been busy with husks and trappings of life and have really missed life itself. For life without God, to one who has known the richness and joy of life with Him, is unthinkable, impossible.

Phillips Brooks

A rainbow ... that smiling daughter of the storm.

Caleb C. Colton

I set My rainbow in the cloud, and it shall be for the sign of the covenant between Me and the earth.

Genesis 9:13

In times of trouble, it is as though the skies darken; thick clouds gather overhead. There is the rumble of thunder; down pours the rain. "Will it ever stop?" Mark Twain was asked. His reputed response: "It always has." And indeed, the rain does stop. The sun peeks through the clouds, and if we are fortunate, we will see the rainbow. Pause each time you see a rainbow, for each rainbow is a reminder of God's promises and care.

A. M.

Trust God where you cannot trace him. Do not try to penetrate the cloud he brings over you; rather look to the bow that is on it. The mystery is God's; the promise is yours.

John Macduff

It is better

It is better to trust in the Lord
Than to put confidence in man.
Better is a dinner of herbs where love is,
Than a fatted calf with hatred.
Better is a little with righteousness,
Than vast revenues without justice.

Better to be of a humble spirit with the lowly,
Than to divide the spoil with the proud.
Better is the poor who walks in his integrity
Than one who is perverse in his lips, and is a fool.

Better is a dry morsel with quietness,
Than a house full of feasting with strife.
The end of a thing is better than its beginning;
The patient in spirit is better than the proud in spirit.

How much better to get wisdom than gold!
For wisdom is better than rubies;
Wisdom is better than strength.

Psalm 118:8; Proverbs 15:17, 16:8, 16:19, 19:1, 17:1; Ecclesiastes 7:8;
Proverbs 16:16, 8:11; Ecclesiastes 9:16

**Many waters cannot quench love,
Nor can the floods drown it.**

Song of Solomon 8:7

Love is not blind. Love is the only thing that sees.

Frank Crane

The heart of him who truly loves is a paradise on earth; he has God in himself, for God is love.

Abbé Hugo Félicité de Lamennais

Love is an image of God, and not a lifeless image, but the living essence of the divine nature which beams full of all goodness.

Martin Luther

In peace, love tunes the shepherd's reed; in war, he mounts the warrior's steed; in halls, in gay attire is seen; in hamlets, dances on the green. Love rules the court, the camp, the grove, and man below, and saints above; for love is heaven, and heaven is love.

Sir Walter Scott

To love another person is to see the face of God.

Victor Hugo

See the light

Then [Saul] fell to the ground, and heard a voice saying to him, "Saul, Saul, why are you persecuting Me?"
And he said, "Who are You, Lord?"
Then the Lord said, "I am Jesus."

Acts 9:4–5

The common expression "to see the light" means to realise the truth, and it is an allusion to the conversion of Paul (earlier known as Saul), one of Christianity's founders. The Bible describes how during his journey to Damascus, intent on persecuting believers, a light shone around him from heaven. The voice from the light told him it was Jesus.

Paul got the message directly from Jesus himself. We may not meet the Lord in such a dramatic way, but we can be assured that when we open our hearts to him, the Light of the world enters.[1]

A. M. [1] John 8:12

As many as received Him [Jesus], to them He gave the right to become children of God, to those who believe in His name.

John 1:12

My prayer

Lord,

Give us hearts never to forget your love, but to dwell therein whatever we do, whether we sleep or wake, live or die, or rise again to the life that is to come.

For your love is eternal life and everlasting rest; for this is life eternal, to know you and your infinite goodness. O let its flame never be quenched in our hearts; let it grow and brighten, until our whole souls are glowing and shining with its light and warmth.

Be our joy, our hope, our strength and life, our shield and shepherd, our portion for ever. For we are happy if we continue in the love with which you have loved us; holy are we when we love you steadfastly.

Therefore, dear Lord, whose name and essence is love, enkindle our hearts, enlighten our understanding, sanctify our wills, and fill all the thoughts of our hearts, for Jesus Christ's sake.

Johann Arndt, adapted

Alpha and Omega.
I am with you always.

Matthew 28:20

For the Christian, heaven is where Jesus is. We do not need to speculate on what heaven will be like. It is enough to know that we will be for ever with Him. When we love anyone with our whole hearts, life begins when we are with that person; it is only in their company that we are really and truly alive. It is so with Christ. In this world our contact with Him is shadowy, for we can only see through a glass darkly. It is spasmodic, for we are poor creatures and cannot live always on the heights. But the best definition of it is to say that heaven is that state where we will always be with Jesus, and where nothing will separate us from Him any more.

William Barclay

His love has no limits,
His grace has no measure,
His power has no boundary
known unto men;
For out of His infinite riches in Jesus
He giveth and giveth and giveth again.

Annie J. Flint

Let us continually offer the sacrifice of praise to God, that is, the fruit of our lips, giving thanks to His name.

Hebrews 13:15

Blessings we enjoy daily, and for the most of them, because they be so common, men forget to pay their praises.—But let not us, because it is a sacrifice so pleasing to him who still protects us, and gives us flowers, and showers, and meat, and content.

Izaak Walton

Let praise begin the day and wake
 The echoes of the morn,
As I my pilgrim journey take
 In strength of life new-born.
To thee my thankful heart does sing,
 God, my exceeding joy;
My morning sacrifice I bring,
 Of love without alloy.
I thank thee who art day by day
 The fountain of all love,
Whence spring the lower streams and they
 That flow from heaven above.
But for thyself I thank thee most,
 In praises o'er and o'er—
The Father, Son, and Holy Ghost,
 Lord for evermore.

Author unknown

Meditate within your heart on your bed, and be still.

Psalm 4:4

Solitude permits the mind to feel.

William Wordsworth

There is hardly ever a complete silence in our soul. God is whispering to us well nigh incessantly. Whenever the sounds of the world die out in the soul, or sink low, then we hear these whisperings of God. He is always whispering to us, only we do not always hear because of the noise, hurry, and distraction which life causes as it rushes on.

Frederick William Faber

Be transformed by the renewing of your mind.

Romans 12:2

God is above, presiding; beneath, sustaining; within, filling.

Hildebert of Lavardin

I have set the LORD always before me;
Because *He is* at my right hand
I shall not be moved.
Therefore my heart is glad,
and my glory rejoices;

Psalm 68:8–9

As your days, so shall your strength be.

Deuteronomy 33:25

Those who do what the LORD tells them are in his care every day, and what he has given them will be theirs forever. They won't be in trouble when times are tough, and they will have enough to live on.

If you do what the LORD wants, he will make sure each step you take is firm. The LORD will hold your hand, and if you stumble, you still won't fall.

Trust the LORD and follow him.

The LORD protects his people, and they can come to him in times of trouble. The LORD helps them and saves them, because they trust in him.

Psalm 37:18–19, 23–24, 34, 39–40 paraphrased

I love to think that God appoints
My portion day by day;
Events of life are in His hand,
And I would only say,
Appoint them in Thine own good time,
And in Thine own best way.

Anna Laetitia Waring

Light is the shadow of God.

Plato

I am the light of the world. He who follows Me shall not walk in darkness, but have the light of life.

John 8:12

The sky is grey today, dark clouds filling the wide expanse. There appears no hope on the horizon. But the sun, even when it is unseen, is always shining, constantly lighting and heating the earth, keeping our planet in orbit. Just so, Jesus, the light of the world, is always with us, loving and caring for us, and keeping us on his path.

A. M.

Walk in the light! And thou shalt find
Thy heart made truly His,
Who dwells in cloudless light enshrined,
In whom no darkness is.
Walk in the light! Thy path shall be
A path, though thorny, bright;
For God, by grace, shall dwell in thee,
And God Himself is light.

Bernard Barton

For in Him we live and move and have our being.

Acts 17:28

But what is heaven, great God,
   compared to thee?
Without thy presence,
   heaven's no heaven to me.

Francis Quarles

No masses of earth can block his vision as he looks over all. With one glance of his intelligence, he sees all that has been, that is, and that is to come.

Anicius Manlius Severinus Boethius

Thou art a sea without a shore,
A sun without a sphere;
Thy time is now and evermore,
   Thy place is everywhere.

John Mason

Now may our Lord Jesus Christ Himself, and our God and Father, who has loved us and given us everlasting consolation and good hope by grace, comfort your hearts and establish you in every good word and work.

2 Thessalonians 2:16–17

Then He arose and rebuked the winds and the sea, and there was a great calm.

Matthew 8:26

[Jesus] condensed it all into one single message of eternal comfort spoken to the disciples on the Sea of Galilee, "It is I, be not afraid."[1] He is the antidote to fear; He is the remedy for trouble; He is the substance and the sum of deliverance.

We should, therefore, rise above fear. Let us keep our eyes fastened upon Him; let us abide continually in Him; let us be content with Him. Let us cling closely to Him and cry, "Therefore will not we fear, though the earth be removed, and though the mountains be carried into the midst of the sea."[2]

Albert Benjamin Simpson. [1]Matthew 14:27 [2]Psalm 46:2

O let me see Your footprints,
    and in them plant mine own;
My hope to follow truly
    is in Your strength alone.
O guide me, call me, draw me,
    uphold me to the end;
And then in Heaven receive me,
    my Savior and my Friend.

John E. Bode

I shall hear in heaven.

Attributed last words of Ludwig van Beethoven

I [Jesus] am the resurrection and the life. He who believes in Me, though he may die, he shall live. And whoever lives and believes in Me shall never die.

John 11:25–26

It is impossible that anything so natural, so necessary and so universal as death, should ever have been designed by Providence as an evil to mankind.

Jonathan Swift

The leaves in autumn do not change colour from the blighting touch of frost, but from the process of natural decay.—They fall when the fruit is ripened and their work is done.—And their splendid colouring is but their graceful and beautiful surrender of life when they have finished their summer offering of service to God and man. And one of the great lessons the fall of the leaf teaches, is this: Do your work well, and then be ready to depart when God shall call.

Tryon Edwards

Let me say thank you

God's goodness hath been great to thee. Let never day nor night unhallowed pass, but still remember what the Lord hath done.

William Shakespeare

Praise the LORD from the earth,
You great sea creatures and all the depths;
Fire and hail, snow and clouds;
Stormy wind, fulfilling His word;
Mountains and all hills;
Fruitful trees and all cedars;
Beasts and all cattle;
Creeping things and flying fowl;
Kings of the earth and all peoples;
Princes and all judges of the earth;
Both young men and maidens;
Old men and children.
Let them praise the name of the LORD,
For His name alone is exalted;
His glory is above the earth and heaven.

Psalm 148:7–13

Gratitude is the inward feeling of kindness received. Thankfulness is the natural impulse to express that feeling. Thanksgiving is the following of that impulse.

Henry Van Dyke

Blessed be the LORD.
There has not failed one word
of all His good promise.

1 Kings 8:56

The sight of powdery flakes on the ground was a puzzle for the people of Israel, hungry and discouraged on their long wilderness journey, but the first taste of manna was a pleasant surprise. It was the beginning of better things to come.

The master of a wedding feast was amazed when he took his first taste of the water miraculously turned to wine. This turned out to be the first of the miracles of Jesus.

One young man went outside of his comfort zone and the reward was finding his soul mate: It was love at first sight for Jacob, son of Isaac, on encountering Rachel.

That first taste of manna, that first sip of wedding wine, that young man's journey remind us that as we look to God for His leading and ask Him for the courage to try something new, we can place our feet confidently on the road ahead.

A. M.   See Exodus 16:13–15, 31; John 2:9–11 and Genesis 29

To trust is to be healed.

Suddenly, a woman who had a flow of blood for twelve years came from behind and touched the hem of His garment. For she said to herself, "If only I may touch His garment, I shall be made well."

Jesus turned around, and when He saw her He said, "Be of good cheer, daughter; your faith has made you well." And the woman was made well from that hour.

Matthew 9:20–22

The good Instructor, the Wisdom, the Word of the Father, who made man, cares for the whole nature of His creature. The all-sufficient Physician of humanity, the Saviour, heals both our body and soul, which are the proper man.

Clement of Alexandria

Let us come in the simplicity of sickness, in the helplessness of want; to trust is to be healed, to touch the hem of his garment is to be whole; but let us keep touching him, for virtue is ever coming from him.

Lady Theodosia Powerscourt

In the beginning was the Word.

And the Word was with God, and the Word was God. He was in the beginning with God. ... And the Word became flesh and dwelt among us.

John 1:1–2,14

The longer you read the Bible, the more you will like it; it will grow sweeter and sweeter; and the more you get into the spirit of it, the more you will get into the spirit of Christ.

William Romaine

The Bible is to us what the star was to the wise men; but if we spend all our time in gazing upon it, observing its motions, and admiring its splendour, without being led to Christ by it, the use of it will be lost to us.

Thomas Adams

We know that the Son of God has come and has given us an understanding, that we may know Him who is true.

1 John 5:20

The eyes of all look expectantly to You.

Psalm 145:15

Be thou my Vision,
O Lord of my heart;
Be all else but naught to me,
    save that thou art
Thou my best thought, by day or by night,
Waking or sleeping, thy presence my light.

Be thou my Wisdom,
    and thou my true Word;
I ever with thee and thou with me, Lord;
Thou my great Father, I thy true son;
Thou in me dwelling, and I with thee one.

High King of heaven, my victory won,
May I reach heaven's joys,
O bright heaven's Sun!
Heart of my own heart, whatever befall,
Still be my Vision, O Ruler of all.

Irish poem of the 8th century

The LORD will command His lovingkindness in the daytime, and in the night His song shall be with me—a prayer to the God of my life.

Psalm 42:8

Lord, You have heard the desire of the humble; You will prepare their heart; You will cause Your ear to hear.

Psalm 10:17

The world measures greatness by money, or eloquence, or intellectual skill, or even by prowess on the field of battle. But here is the Lord's standard: "Whosoever shall humble himself as this little child, the same is the greatest in the kingdom of heaven."[1]

John Henry Jowett. [1]Matthew 18:4 KJV

"I long to accomplish great and noble tasks, but it is my chief duty to accomplish humble tasks as though they were great and noble. The world is moved along, not only by the mighty shoves of its heroes, but also by the aggregate of the tiny pushes of each honest worker."— Thus wrote Helen Keller, blind, deaf and dumb from infancy.

A.M.

If you are humble, nothing will touch you, neither praise nor disgrace, because you know what you are.

Mother Teresa

Come to me, all you who labour and are heavily burdened, and I will give you rest.

Take my yoke upon you, and learn from me, for I am gentle and lowly in heart; and you will find rest for your souls. For my yoke is easy, and my burden is light.

Matthew 11:28–30 (WEB)

The camel at the close of day
Kneels down upon the sandy plain
To have his burden lifted off,
And rest to gain.

My soul, thou too shouldst to thy knees
When daylight draweth to a close,
And let thy Master lift thy load,
And grant repose.

Else how canst thou tomorrow meet,
With all tomorrow's work to do,
If thou thy burden all the night
Dost carry through?

The camel kneels at break of day
To have his guide replace his load;
Then rises up anew to take
The desert road.

So thou shouldst kneel at morning's dawn,
That God may give the daily care;
Assured that He no load too great
Will make thee bear.

Anna Temple

When I am weak, then I am strong.

I pleaded with the Lord three times that [this affliction] might depart from me. And He said to me, "My grace is sufficient for you, for My strength is made perfect in weakness."

Therefore most gladly I will rather boast in my infirmities, that the power of Christ may rest upon me. For when I am weak, then I am strong.

2 Corinthians 12:8–10

We may not have the strength we would like; our sight may be dimmed, or our hearing impaired; physical or mental challenges may impose very real limitations. But there is no design flaw. God, in his great love, has equipped each of us for our own particular life's journey. It was a deaf Beethoven who composed some of our greatest music; a disabled Walter Scott and a blind Milton who gave us some of our greatest literature; the deaf Goya some of our greatest art. If one ability eludes us, let us seek another.

A. M.

The end of all is love,
And the crown of love is peace.

Emma Marshall

Though I speak with the tongues of men and of angels, but have not love, I have become sounding brass or a clanging cymbal.

And though I have the gift of prophecy, and understand all mysteries and all knowledge, and though I have all faith, so that I could remove mountains, but have not love, I am nothing.

And though I bestow all my goods to feed the poor, and though I give my body to be burned, but have not love, it profits me nothing.

And now abide faith, hope, love, these three; but the greatest of these is love.

1 Corinthians 13:1–3,13

They are the true disciples of Christ, not who know most, but who love most.

Frederick Spanheim

Love is not getting, but giving. Love is ... the best thing in the world, and the thing that lives the longest.

Henry Van Dyke

Why are you cast down, O my soul?

As the deer pants for the water brooks,
So pants my soul for You, O God.
My soul thirsts for God, for the living God.
When shall I come and appear before God?

My tears have been my food day and night,
While they continually say to me,
"Where is your God?"

When I remember these things,
I pour out my soul within me.
For I used to go with the multitude;
I went with them to the house of God,
With the voice of joy and praise,
With a multitude that kept a pilgrim feast.

Why are you cast down, O my soul?
And why are you disquieted within me?
Hope in God, for I shall yet praise Him
For the help of His countenance.

Psalm 42:1–5

The LORD is good to those who wait for Him, to the soul who seeks Him.

Lamentations 3:25

Blessed are those who hunger and thirst
   for righteousness,
     For they shall be filled.
Blessed are the pure in heart,
   For they shall see God.

Matthew 5:6,8

I know that, if any of you have tasted the sweetness of Christ, you would be content to abide in him for eternity.

Robert Murray M'Cheyne

Filling up our time *with* and *for* God is the way to rise up and lie down in peace.

David Brainerd

The capital of heaven is the heart in which Jesus Christ is enthroned as King.

Sadhu Sundar Singh

O God, who art the truth, make me one with thee in everlasting love! I am often weary of reading and weary of hearing; in thee alone is the sum of all my desires. Let all teachers be silent, let the whole creation be dumb before thee, and do thou only speak to my soul.

Thomas à Kempis

Written in light

Great is our Lord, and mighty in power;
His understanding is infinite.
He counts the number of the stars;
He calls them all by name.

Psalm 147:5,4

If the stars should appear one night in a thousand years, how would men believe and adore; and preserve for many generations the remembrance of the city of God which had been shown! But every night come out these envoys of beauty, and light the universe with their admonishing smile.

Ralph Waldo Emerson

When the blazing sun is gone,
When he nothing shines upon,
Then you show your little light,
Twinkle, twinkle, all the night.
Then the traveller in the dark
Thanks you for your tiny spark,
How could he see where to go,
If you did not twinkle so?

Jane Taylor

There they stand, the innumerable stars, shining in order like a living hymn, written in light.

Nathaniel Parker Willis

Clean up your act

Go home and wash up. Clean up your act. Sweep your lives clean of your evildoings so I don't have to look at them any longer. Say no to wrong.

Isaiah 1:16 MSG

Zaccheus was a tax collector—never a popular job—and to top things off, honesty was not too high on his priority list. Nonetheless, he went out of his way to hear what Jesus had to say, and Jesus in turn went out of His way to meet with him. Zaccheus got the message loud and clear that he should stop fiddling the books and cheating the people from whom he was collecting taxes. He stopped in his tracks, made a pledge, and paid back over and above what he had stolen.[1]

What would God want me to stop doing? Is there a sin, a bad habit? God help me to make the changes that I need.

A. M.   [1]See Luke 19:2–10.

Draw near to God and He will draw near to you. Cleanse your hands, you sinners; and purify your hearts, you double-minded.

James 4:8

The upright will live in your presence.

Psalm 140:13

You have made us for yourself and our hearts are restless until they find their rest in you.

Augustine of Hippo

O Christ, in Thee my soul hath found,
And found in Thee alone,
The peace, the joy I sought so long,
The bliss till now unknown.

I sighed for rest and happiness,
I yearned for them, not Thee;
But while I passed my Saviour by,
His love laid hold on me.

Now none but Christ can satisfy,
None other name for me;
There's love, and life, and lasting joy,
Lord Jesus, found in Thee.

Author unknown

There come times when I have nothing more to tell God. If I were to continue to pray in words, I would have to repeat what I have already said. At such times it is wonderful to say to God, "May I be in Thy presence, Lord? I have nothing more to say to Thee, but I do love to be in Thy presence."

Ole Hallesby

God is your true friend and will always give you the counsel and comfort you need.

François de la Mothe-Fénelon

Please inquire of God, that we may know whether the journey on which we go will be prosperous.

Judges 18:5

The deeper we go down into the valley of decision the higher we must rise ... into the mount of prayer.

Peter Taylor Forsythe

God's might to direct me,
God's power to protect me,
God's wisdom for learning,
God's eye for discerning,
God's ear for my hearing,
God's Word for my clearing.

St Patrick

The strength and happiness of a man consists in finding out the way in which God is going, and going in that way, too.

Henry Ward Beecher

Your ears shall hear a word behind you, saying, "This is the way, walk in it," whenever you turn to the right hand or whenever you turn to the left.

Isaiah 30:21

We hear them speaking in our own tongues the wonderful works of God.

Acts 2:11

Language is the light of the mind.

John Stuart Mill

Language is an anonymous, collective and unconscious art; the result of the creativity of thousands of generations.

Edward Sapir

Language is the amber in which a thousand precious thoughts have been safely embedded and preserved.

Richard Chenevix Trench

You live a new life for every new language you speak.

Czech proverb

If you talk to a man in a language he understands, that goes to his head. If you talk to him in his language, that goes to his heart.

Nelson Mandela

You are worth as many men as you know languages.

Attributed to Charles V

A word fitly spoken is like apples of gold
In settings of silver.

Proverbs 25:11

My prayer

Trust in the LORD, and do good;
Dwell in the land, and feed on His faithfulness.
Delight yourself also in the LORD,
And He shall give you the desires of your heart.

Psalm 37:3–4

Dear Jesus,

I don't know what the future holds for me, but I put that future in your hands. Thank you for the many promises you have given that encourage me to trust you. Help me to have faith as I begin this new year, to be fully persuaded that what you have promised, you will also perform.[1]

No matter what life has in store, may I stay close to you and draw comfort from the knowledge that nothing can separate me from your love.[2]

May I walk in truth, in love, in wisdom, and most of all with you.

[1] *Romans 4:21;* [2] *Romans 8:38–39*

**How great are His signs,
And how mighty His wonders!**

Daniel 4:3

The universe is one of God's thoughts.

Friedrich Schiller

In the vast and the minute, we see
The unambiguous footsteps of the God
Who gives its lustre to the insect's wing,
And wheels his throne upon the rolling worlds.

William Cowper

What is a miracle? I know of nothing else but miracles. Every hour of the light and the dark is a miracle. Every cubic inch of space is a miracle. Every square yard of the surface of the earth is spread with the same; every foot underground swarms with the same. The sea is a continual miracle. The fishes that swim, the rocks, the motions of the waves, the ships with men in them. What stranger miracles are there?

Walt Whitman

The wise man's eyes are in his head, he sees with an inner sight, and discovers God everywhere at work.

Charles Haddon Spurgeon

The fountain of life

He said to me, "It is done! I am the Alpha and the Omega, the Beginning and the End. I will give of the fountain of the water of life freely to him who thirsts."

Revelation 21:6

Sages of the earth,

Christ is the key of your problems, the completion of that philosophy which you resume without ceasing, but never finish;

Troubled spirits, he is your peace;

Lovers of wealth, he is your true treasure;

Men, he is the word that solves the enigma of life, and conquers the power of death.

He alone binds us to the author of our being, and to universal order.

Alexandre Rodolphe Vinet

I believe there is no one lovelier, deeper, more sympathetic and more perfect than Jesus—not only is there no one else like him, but there could never be anyone like him.

Fyodor Dostoevsky

The person you are now, the person you have been, the person you will be—this person God has chosen as beloved.

William Countryman

Even the sparrow has found a home,
And the swallow a nest for herself,
Where she may lay her young—
Even Your altars, O LORD of hosts.

Psalm 84:3

God's love is not drawn out by our loveableness, but wells up, like an artesian spring, from the depths of his nature.

Alexander Maclaren

Whenever a person says to me: "My problem is that I do not love the Lord enough", I usually respond: "No... your problem is that you don't know how much the Lord loves you."

Selwyn Hughes

To the frightened, God is friendly; to the poor in spirit, he is forgiving; to the ignorant, considerate; to the weak, gentle; to the stranger, hospitable.

Aiden Wilson Tozer

Can a mother forget the baby at her breast and have no compassion on the child she has borne? Though she may forget, I will not forget you!

Isaiah 49:15 NIV

Hear my cry, O God;
Attend to my prayer.

From the end of the earth I will cry to You,
When my heart is overwhelmed;
Lead me to the rock that is higher than I.

Psalm 61:1–2

Should we feel at times disheartened and discouraged, a confiding thought, a simple movement of heart toward God will renew our powers. Whatever he may demand of us, he will give us at the moment the strength and the courage that we need.

François de la Mothe-Fénelon

From one disaster after another he delivers you; no matter what the calamity, the evil can't touch you.

Job 5:19 MSG

Grant, O God, that amidst all the discouragements, difficulties, dangers, distress and darkness of this mortal life, I may depend upon your mercy and on this build my hopes, as on a sure foundation. Let your infinite mercy in Christ Jesus deliver me from despair.

Thomas Wilson

This is the testimony: that God has given us eternal life, and this life is in His Son.

1 John 5:11

Great discoveries and grand journeys of exploration are stories of dedication and passion, determination and perseverance. The search goes on for cures and solutions; for hidden places above the stars, to hidden wonders of the deep.

There is another search, closer to home: The search within the self for peace of mind, contentment of heart, purpose for living, hope for eternity. Happy indeed are those who discover Christ, for he fills the gaping space in the human heart.

It has been said that discovering Christ is the greatest adventure of life.—And it is not a one-time discovery. Each day can bring another precious find. Getting to know him through prayer, reading and meditation can become our greatest treasure, as Paul wrote, "For me, indeed, to live is Christ."[1]

A. M. *[1]Philippians 1:21*

I remember two things; that I am a great sinner and that Christ is a great Saviour.

John Newton

It is good for me to draw near to God;

I have put my trust in the Lord GOD,
That I may declare all Your works.

Psalm 73:28

Lord,

Although sometimes it's hard, deep in my heart I recognise that I can be thankful even for the struggles in my life and the things that are difficult, because they force me to turn to you for help. You make things easier to understand and give me a focal place to trust. When I turn my heart to you, I receive hope.

Without difficulties, disappointments, and failures, I would not know as much about your compassion, your understanding and your forgiveness, and I wouldn't be able to pass them on to others.

And so, even if it be through tears, I thank you for the things you bring my way to make me more dependent on you. Thank you for keeping me close to you.

Enduring kindness

"For the mountains shall depart
And the hills be removed,
But My kindness shall not depart from you,
Nor shall My covenant of peace be removed,"
Says the LORD, who has mercy on you.

Isaiah 54:10

I will hear what God the LORD will speak,
For He will speak peace
To His people.
LORD, You will establish peace for us,
For You have also done all our works in us.
Let Your mercies come also to me, O LORD—
Your salvation according to Your word.

Psalm 85:8; Isaiah 26:12; Psalm 119:41

O God,
you are the unsearchable abyss of peace,
The ineffable sea of love,
And the fountain of blessings.
Water us with plenteous streams
From the riches of your grace;
And from the sweet springs of your kindness,
Make us children of quietness and heirs of
peace.

Clement of Alexandria

He who is faithful in what is least is faithful also in much.

Luke 16:10

Be joyful, and keep your faith and your creed. Do the little things that you have seen me do and heard about.

St David

The creation of a thousand forests is in one acorn.

Ralph Waldo Emerson

"Take your needle, my child, and work at your pattern; it will come out a rose by and by." Life is like that; one stitch at a time taken patiently, and the pattern will come out all right, like embroidery.

Oliver Wendell Holmes

I am only one, but still I am one. I cannot do everything, but still I can do something; and because I cannot do everything, I will not refuse to do something I can do.

Edward Everett Hale

When you walk with God, you get where he's going.

Author unknown

God is my strength and power,
And He makes my way perfect.

2 Samuel 22:33

When Jesus sent His followers out on the road, they didn't really know what to expect of this first journey. They could have easily missed the opportunity, afraid of the unforeseen consequences. But they went out as instructed, returning later jubilant from their road trip: "The seventy returned with joy."

Based on Luke 10:1, 17

"Be strong, all you people of the land," says the LORD, "and work; for I am with you."

Haggai 2:4

Lord Jesus Christ, the Way by which we travel; show me thyself, the Truth that we must walk in; and be in me the Life that lifts up to God, our journey's ending.

Frederick B. MacNutt

**Behold, now is the accepted time;
behold, now is the day of salvation.**

2 Corinthians 6:2

The golden moments in the stream of life rush past us, and we see nothing but sand; the angels come to visit us, and we only know them when they are gone.

George Eliot

A brilliantly-coloured butterfly alights on a rock in the garden. We rush to get our camera; the butterfly flies away. Our child's first steps are photographed, but did we hold and give him a big hug? We count the days to our vacation, not noticing the daily glories of the sunrise and sunset from our bedroom window.

Not a minute should be ignored, for it can never be regained. In the words of poet Thich Nhat Hanh: "People sacrifice the present for the future. But life is available only in the present. That is why we should walk in such a way that every step can bring us to the here and the now."

A. M.

The present moment is always a season which may be used or may be neglected, but which can never be recalled.

Canon Wynne

In quietness and confidence shall be your strength.

Isaiah 30:15

Stillness of spirit is like the canvas for the Holy Spirit to draw his various graces upon.

John Love

God is a tranquil Being, and abides in a tranquil eternity. So must thy spirit become a tranquil and clear little pool, wherein the serene light of God can be mirrored.

Gerhard Tersteegen

Lift up my soul, O Lord,
   above the weary round
   of harassing thoughts,
   to your eternal presence.
Lift up my mind
   to the pure, bright, serene
   atmosphere of your presence,
   that I may breathe freely,
   and rest there in your love.
From there, surrounded by your peace,
   may I return to do or to bear
   whatever shall best please you,
     O blessed Lord.

Edward Pusey, adapted

Each one special

Are not two sparrows sold for a copper coin? And not one of them falls to the ground apart from your Father's will. But the very hairs of your head are all numbered. Do not fear therefore; you are of more value than many sparrows.

Matthew 10:29–31

I sit here and consider the lilies, and behold the sparrows, and know that as the Lord is taking care of them, he will certainly take care of us. Whenever one sparrow falls to the ground, our heavenly Father knows that it has fallen. How much more is he looking after us! Each of us is special to him.

Author unknown

Why should I feel discouraged,
    why should the shadows come,
Why should my heart be lonely,
    and long for heaven and home,
When Jesus is my portion?
My constant friend is He:
His eye is on the sparrow,
    and I know He watches me.

Civilla D. Martin

You are God

Before the mountains were brought forth,
Or ever You had formed the earth
   and the world,
Even from everlasting to everlasting,
You are God.

Psalm 90:2

Dear Lord,

How brief is our span of life compared with the time since you created the universe. How tiny we are compared with the enormity of your universe. How trivial are our concerns compared with the complexity of your universe. How stupid we are compared with the genius of your creation.

Yet during every minute and every second of our lives you are present, within and around us. You give your attention to each and every one of us. Our concerns are your concerns. And you are infinitely patient with our stupidity. I thank you with all my heart—knowing that my thanks are worthless compared to your greatness.

Fulbert of Chartres

So teach us to number our days,
That we may gain a heart of wisdom.

Psalm 90:12

According to researchers, on average it takes 66 days to form a habit. Add some new activity into your daily routine—such as taking a walk after dinner, eating fruit in the mid-afternoon, or having five minutes of quiet meditation when you wake in the morning—and if you're still doing it two months later, it is likely you'll be doing it automatically.

Did you make a resolution at the start of this year? If so, and you've been able to keep it up, you have successfully integrated a new feature into your daily living. Today is the 66th day. If you haven't yet, it's never too late to begin.

A. M.

We think very little of time present; we anticipate the future, as being too slow, and with a view to hasten it onward, we recall the past to stay it as too swiftly gone. We are so thoughtless, that we thus wander through the hours that are not here, regardless only of the moment that is actually our own.—To eternity itself there is no other handle than the present moment.

Blaise Pascal

...And many other women

There were also women looking on from afar ... who also followed [Jesus] and ministered to Him when He was in Galilee, and many other women who came up with Him to Jerusalem.

Mark 15:40–41

During the early days of Christianity, the fledgling movement suffered considerable persecution. Gatherings of any number could draw the attention of the authorities, yet even under these circumstances, Mary, the mother of a follower named John Mark, opened her house for prayer meetings.[1] She was presumably a widow, as the biblical text refers to the house as her own, not her husband's. She knew the risks, but that did not stop her opening her doors. In doing so, she was not only supporting the new church, but also her own son, and stands as yet another example of the generosity and bravery of women.

A. M. [1]*Acts 12:12*

Woman was taken out of man; not out of his head to top him, nor out of his feet to be trampled underfoot; but out of his side to be equal to him, under his arm to be protected and near his heart to be loved.

Matthew Henry

**God has two dwellings:
one in heaven, and the other in a meek
and thankful heart.**

Izaak Walton

The LORD is my strength and my shield;
My heart trusted in Him, and I am helped;
Therefore my heart greatly rejoices,
And with my song I will praise Him.

Psalm 28:7

Joy is the echo of God's life within us.

Joseph Marmion

Gratitude is the memory of the heart; therefore
forget not to say often, I have all I have ever
enjoyed.

Lydia M. Child

A map tells us where we're going and a
compass tells us the direction to travel. Owen
Young gives this directional guidance: "Praise,
more divine than prayer; prayer points our
ready path to heaven; praise is already there."

A. M.

Enter into His gates with thanksgiving,
And into His courts with praise.
Be thankful to Him, and bless His name.

Psalm 100:4

In all these things we are more than conquerors through Him who loved us.

Romans 8:37

I arise today
Through God's mighty strength,
His power to uphold me,
His wisdom to guide me,
And his hand to guard me.

I arise today,
Through Christ's mighty strength,
Through his death and resurrection,
Through the Spirit's empowering,
Through the presence of angels
and the love of the saints,
Through the threefold Trinity
to protect me from evil.

St Patrick

Obstacles cannot crush me. Every obstacle yields to stern resolve. He who is fixed to a star does not change his mind.

Leonardo da Vinci

Keep a green branch in your heart and the singing bird will come.

Chinese proverb

This is the victory that has overcome the world—our faith.

1 John 5:4

I will give you rain in its season, the land shall yield its produce, and the trees of the field shall yield their fruit.

Leviticus 26:4

Four friends were reminiscing over a drink. It so happened that during the course of the year, each in turn had passed through a picturesque valley some distance away, well known for its pear orchards.

The first friend had passed through the area in winter. He described his disappointment at driving through a bleak landscape of twisted, bare trees. The second friend disagreed with his negative appraisal of the countryside; the trees had been covered with green buds. The third had passed through a little later in the year, and during his visit the trees had been filled with sweet fragrant blossoms.

The last friend had seen something different from all of them. "The orchards were heavy with ripe golden fruit!" In fact, the sweet pear cider they were drinking had been bottled in that valley.

Sometimes we think we know the whole picture, but we are only seeing a part, just as each of the friends had only seen one season of life in the valley. It may seem like winter in our lives, but the promise of spring, the beauty of summer and the fulfilment of autumn await us.

Retold

The light of day

Unto us a Child is born,
Unto us a Son is given;
And the government will be
upon His shoulder.
And His name will be called
Wonderful, Counselor, Mighty God,
Everlasting Father, Prince of Peace.

Isaiah 9:6

In the words of Bettie J. Eadie, near-death survivor and author of *Embraced by the Light*: "Heaven in all its glory could be summed up in one word: Christ. He is the light of creation, the joy of all life, and above all, the deepest love of our souls. To embrace Him is to embrace the meaning of life and the eternal power of God."

Joyful, joyful, we adore Thee,
God of glory, Lord of love;
Hearts unfold like flowers before Thee,
opening to the sun above.
Melt the clouds of sin and sadness;
drive the dark of doubt away;
Giver of immortal gladness,
fill us with the light of day!

Henry Van Dyke

Friendship is one of the sweetest joys of life.

Charles Haddon Spurgeon

A friend loves at all times. Two are better than one, because they have a good reward for their labor. For if they fall, one will lift up his companion. But woe to him who is alone when he falls, for he has no one to help him up.

Again, if two lie down together, they will keep warm; but how can one be warm alone? Though one may be overpowered by another, two can withstand him. And a threefold cord is not quickly broken.

Ointment and perfume delight the heart, and the sweetness of a man's friend gives delight by hearty counsel. You use steel to sharpen steel, and one friend sharpens another. A man who has friends must himself be friendly.

Proverbs 17:17 KJV; Ecclesiastes 4:9–12 (NKJ); Ecclesiastes 6:14–16 (NKJ); Proverbs 27:9, 17 (NKJ); Proverbs 18:24 (NKJ)

Friendship improves happiness, and abates misery, by doubling our joy, and dividing our grief.

Joseph Addison

Speak, Lord, I'm listening.

The Lord came and stood there, calling as at the other times, "Samuel! Samuel!" Then Samuel said, "Speak, for your servant is listening."

1 Samuel 3:10

Heavenly Father,

Thank you for another fresh start today. The first thing I want to do with this day is share it with you. Before I do anything else, I want to sit right here, at your feet, and listen to what you have to tell me today. If you want to tell me anything, here I am, Lord. You have my undivided attention. If you have any direction, counsel, guidance, words of wisdom—or even words of love, here I am. I'm listening.

This is my favourite part of each brand-new day, this time in the morning when I can put aside the cares of life to listen to you and find the strength I need to make it through the day. Thank you for this time.

Hearts and hands.

There is a wonderful law of nature that the three things we crave most in life—happiness, freedom and peace of mind—are always attained by giving them to someone else.

Peyton Conway March

You learn to speak by speaking, to study by studying, to run by running, to work by working; and just so, you learn to love by loving. All those who think to learn in any other way deceive themselves.

Francis de Sales

There is no difficulty that enough love will not conquer, no disease that enough love will not heal. No door that enough love will not open, no gulf that enough love will not bridge. No wall that enough love will not throw down, no sin that enough love will not redeem. It makes no difference how deeply seated may be the trouble, how hopeless the outlook, how muddled the tangle, how great the mistake. Sufficient love will dissolve it all.

Emmet Fox

An inheritance in light

Giving thanks to the Father who has qualified us to be partakers of the inheritance of the saints in the light.

Colossians 1:12

What is this inheritance?

It is a tearless state: God himself will wipe away all tears. *Now* He puts them into His bottle; *then* He will stop their flow.

But it is also a place. There is a heavenly "city."[1] This suggests the idea of locality, society, security; there will be sweet companionship.

It is a "fold" where all the sheep of the Good Shepherd will be safe: He who brought them there will guard them. It is a "kingdom:" and there the glory of God will be revealed. It is a "feast:" and there the bounties of the great Giver will be enjoyed. It is a "garden," an Eden, a paradise: and there will bloom, in immortal freshness, the most beautiful and fragrant flowers.

It is an inheritance in light.

Rev Canon Money, adapted. [1]*Revelation 21*

Now you are light in the Lord. Walk as children of light.

Ephesians 5:8

Remembering St Patrick

Go therefore and make disciples of all the nations, baptizing them in the name of the Father and of the Son and of the Holy Spirit.

Matthew 28:19

Patrick (373–465 AD), the patron saint of Ireland, is said to have used a shamrock—a three-leaf clover—to explain the three parts of the Godhead: God the Father, Jesus His Son and the Holy Spirit.

Patrick would hold up a shamrock and challenge his hearers, "Is it one leaf or three?"

"It is both one leaf and three," was their reply.

"And so it is with God," he would say.

Retold

All glory to the Father,
The unbegotten One;
All honour be to Jesus,
His sole begotten Son;
And to the Holy Spirit—
The perfect Trinity.
Let all the worlds give answer,
"Amen—so let it be."

St Columba

"With everlasting kindness
I will have mercy on you,"
says the LORD, your Redeemer.

Isaiah 54:8

When on my aching, burdened heart
   My sins lie heavily,
My pardon speak, new peace impart,
   In love remember me.

Thomas Haweis

I look to Thee in every need,
And never look in vain;
I feel Thy touch, Eternal Love,
   And all is well again:
The thought of Thee is mightier far
Than sin and pain and sorrow are.

Samuel Longfellow

Bless the LORD, O my soul ...
Who forgives all your iniquities,
Who heals all your diseases,
Who redeems your life from destruction,
Who crowns you with lovingkindness and
tender mercies,
Who satisfies your mouth with good things,
So that your youth is renewed like the eagle's.

Psalm 103:2–5

To see God in everything makes life the greatest adventure there is.

Author unknown

For this reason I bow my knees to the Father of our Lord Jesus Christ, from whom the whole family in heaven and earth is named, that He would grant you, according to the riches of His glory, to be strengthened with might through His Spirit in the inner man, that Christ may dwell in your hearts through faith; that you, being rooted and grounded in love, may be able to comprehend with all the saints what is the width and length and depth and height—to know the love of Christ which passes knowledge; that you may be filled with all the fullness of God.

Now to Him who is able to do exceedingly abundantly above all that we ask or think, according to the power that works in us, to Him be glory in the church by Christ Jesus to all generations, forever and ever. Amen.

Ephesians 3:14–21

The gardens of kindness never fade.

Greek proverb

Whatever a man sows, that he will also reap.

Galatians 6:7

Wherever there is a human being there is a chance for kindness.

Lucius Annaeus Seneca

Life is made up, not of great sacrifices or duties, but of little things, in which smiles, and kindnesses, and small obligations, given habitually, are what win and preserve the heart and secure comfort.

Sir Humphrey Davy

In this world of hurry, and work,
and sudden end,
If a thought comes quick of doing kindness
to a friend,
Do it that very minute;
don't put it off, don't wait;
What's the use of doing a kindness,
if you do it a day too late?

Author unknown

God's got you covered. He's watching out for you, and he guarantees that all decisions made for love will be rewarded.

Author unknown

Praising your splendid Name

Blessed are you, GOD of Israel, our father from of old and forever.

To you, O GOD, belong the greatness and the might, the glory, the victory, the majesty, the splendor; Yes! Everything in heaven, everything on earth; the kingdom all yours!

You've raised yourself high over all. Riches and glory come from you, you're ruler over all; You hold strength and power in the palm of your hand to build up and strengthen all.

And here we are, O God, our God, giving thanks to you, praising your splendid Name.

1 Chronicles 29:10–13 MSG

To God the Father, who first loved us,
   and made us accepted in the beloved:

To God the Son, who loved us, and washed us from our sins in his own blood:

To God the Holy Ghost, who sheds the love of God abroad in our hearts:

Be all love and all glory, for all time and for eternity.

Thomas Ken

A star is beautiful;

It affords pleasure, not from what it is to do, or to give, but simply by being what it is. It befits the heavens; it has congruity with the mighty space in which it dwells. It has repose; no force disturbs its eternal peace. It has freedom; no obstruction lies between it and infinity.

Thomas Carlyle

Teach me your mood, O patient stars!
  Who climb each night the ancient sky,
Leaving on space no shade, no scars,
  No trace of age, no fear to die.

Ralph Waldo Emerson

Look at the night skies: Who do you think made all this? Who marches this army of stars out each night, counts them off, calls each by name - so magnificent! so powerful! - and never overlooks a single one?

Isaiah 40:26 MSG

Creator of the stars of night,
thy people's everlasting light,
O Christ, thou Saviour of us all,
we pray thee, hear us when we call.

Latin hymnal

Restored with clear sight

Then [Jesus] came to Bethsaida; and they brought a blind man to Him, and begged Him to touch him. So He took the blind man by the hand and led him out of the town. And when He had spit on his eyes and put His hands on him, He asked him if he saw anything. And he looked up and said, "I see men like trees, walking." Then He put His hands on his eyes again and made him look up. And he was restored and saw everyone clearly.

Mark 8:22–25

We don't always understand why things are out of focus. Hours turn into days, and days into weeks, and it seems there is a never-ending stream of things to take care of. Then one morning we wake up, and we just feel at a loss. Where are we heading? It's hard to keep going when our vision is blurred.

The solution is there waiting for us: First of all, step aside with Jesus, "out of town" in spirit if not in body. Focus on him. Have patience; the answer doesn't always come right away, but in those quiet moments, resting in prayer and meditation, he will restore our vision.

A. M.

Go in peace. The presence of the LORD be with you on your way.

Judges 18:6

There remains therefore a rest for the people of God. For he who has entered His rest has himself also ceased from his works as God did from His. Let us therefore be diligent to enter that rest.

Hebrews 4:9–11

All work and no rest takes the spring and bound out of the most vigorous life.—Time spent in judicious resting is not time wasted, but time gained.

M. B. Grier

Through the week we go down into the valleys of care and shadow.—Our Sabbaths should be hills of light and joy in God's presence; and so as time rolls by we shall go on from mountain top to mountain top, till at last we catch the glory of the gate, and enter in to go no more out forever.

Henry Ward Beecher

Truly God is good.

Psalm 73:1

There are many who say,
"Who will show us any good?"
LORD, lift up the light of Your countenance upon us.
For You are my lamp, O LORD;
The LORD shall enlighten my darkness.

Psalm 4:6; 2 Samuel 22:29

Darkness is fled.—Now flowers unfold their beauties to the sun, and blushing, kiss the beam he sends to wake them.

Richard Brinsley Sheridan

If the sun of God's countenance shines upon me, I may well be content with the rain of adversity.

Author unknown

What we count the ills of life are often blessings in disguise, resulting in good to us in the end.—Though for the present not joyous but grievous, yet, if received in a right spirit, they work out fruits of righteousness for us at last.

Matthew Henry

The very word "God" suggests care, kindness, goodness; and the idea of God in His infinity, is infinite care, infinite kindness, infinite goodness.

Henry Ward Beecher

Each and every one

What is man that You are mindful of him,
And the son of man that You visit him?
For You have crowned him
   with glory and honor.

Psalm 8:4–5

As small as we may feel, as insignificant as we may judge ourselves to be in the great scope of the world and history, God thinks about each of us. He "is mindful" of us. The God who set the great creation into motion, the same God knows the very hairs of our heads,[1] knows our thoughts and plans,[2] knows our secret sorrows just as He knows our wishes.[3] We are not alone in the universe; God knows and loves me and you.[4]

A sense of wonder accompanies this realisation of the distinct love of God for each of us, each solitary individual. We can surely conclude along with David, "O Lord, our Lord, how excellent is Your name in all the earth!"[5]

A. M.   [1]*Luke 12:7;* [2]*Hebrews 4:12;* [3]*Psalm 38:9;* [4]*John 3:16;* [5]*Psalm 8:9*

Resolved

From there you will seek the Lord your God, and you will find Him if you seek Him with all your heart and with all your soul.

Deuteronomy 4:29

Resolved, to live with all my might while I do live.

Resolved, never to lose one moment of time, to improve it in the most profitable way I can.

Resolved, never to do anything which I should despise or think meanly in another.

Resolved, never to do anything out of revenge.

Resolved, never to do anything which I should be afraid to do if it were the last hour of my life.

Arthur James Balfour

They will be my people, and I will be their God. I will give them singleness of heart and action, so that they will always fear me and that all will then go well for them and for their children after them.

Jeremiah 32:38–39 NIV

The LORD is my shepherd.

Psalm 23:1

So we, Your people and sheep of Your pasture,
Will give You thanks forever;
We will show forth Your praise to all
generations.

Psalm 79:13

O our Saviour! Of ourselves we cannot love you, cannot follow you, cannot become one with you, but you came down that we might love you. You ascended that we might follow you. You bound us close to you that we might be held fast to you.

Since you have loved us, make us love you. Since you found us when we were lost, be yourself the way, that we may find you and be found in you, our only hope and our everlasting joy.

Edward Pusey

This hope we have as an anchor of the soul, both sure and steadfast.

Hebrews 6:19

We do not steady the ship by fixing the anchor on anything that is inside the vessel. The anchorage must be outside of the ship. And so the soul does not rest on what it sees in itself, but on what it sees in the character of God, the certainty of his truth, the impossibility of his falsehood.

Dr Thomas Chalmers, adapted

I've an anchor safe and sure,
    that can evermore endure.
[I withstand] the tempest's shock,
    for my anchor grips the rock.
Through the storm I safely ride,
    till the turning of the tide.
For in Christ I can be bold,
    I've an anchor that shall hold.

And it holds, my anchor holds;
Blow your wildest, then, O gale,
On my bark so small and frail;
By His grace I shall not fail;
For my anchor holds,
    my anchor holds.

William Clark Martin

The Healer

Let your great Physician heal you in his own way. Only follow his directions, and take the medicine which he prescribes, and then quietly leave the result with him.

Edward Payson

The Son of God came, as the great Physician of the soul, to heal all who were diseased, to bind up the brokenhearted, to give sight to the blind, to set at liberty those who are bruised, and to proclaim the acceptable year of the Lord.[1]

My soul, do you know Jesus as your physician? Has he examined you in your illness and told you his diagnosis? And are you, through his mercy, restored to health? Have you heard him ask the tender question, "Will you be made whole?"[2] And have you rejoiced to come under his care?

What is more, has Jesus freely given you his remedies, without payment, without money and without price? Tell every poor soul, Jesus is the beloved Physician, who visits the poor and the needy, and heals every kind of sickness and all types of disease among the people, and he has healed me.

Robert Hawker, adapted. [1] *Isaiah 61:1–2;* [2] *John 5:6*

Heaven, the treasury of everlasting joy.

William Shakespeare

Jesus taught us to pray, "Our Father in heaven."[1]—And that's why heaven is heaven. God is there.

[1]*Luke 11:2*

The happiness of mankind is not to be found in this life; it is a flower that grows in the garden of eternity, and to be expected in its full fruition only in that life which is to come.

Matthew Hale

This is the house of complaints, heaven is the house of praise; this is the house of sorrow, heaven is the house of joy; this is the house of pilgrimage, heaven is the house of our abode; this is the house of our misery, heaven is the house of our eternal solace, when there shall be no end of our joy and rejoicing. Wait, and then, for behold he comes with 10,000 of his saints.

Andrew Gray

If God hath made this world so fair, where sin and death abound, how beautiful, beyond compare, will paradise be found.

James Montgomery

Beware what earth calls happiness;
beware all joys,
but joys that never can expire.

Edward Young

Take heed, and beware of all covetousness; for a man's life does not consist in the abundance of his possessions.

Luke 12:15 (RSV)

Let temporal things serve your use, but the eternal be the subject of your desire.

Thomas à Kempis

He who provides for this life, but takes no care for eternity, is wise for a moment, but a fool forever.

John Tillotson

Lift up our hearts, O Christ, above the false shows of things, above laziness and fear, above selfishness and covetousness, above whim and fashion, up to the everlasting Truth that you are; that so we may live joyfully and freely, in the faith that you are our King and our Saviour, our Example and our Judge, and that, so long as we are loyal to you, all will ultimately be well.

Charles Kingsley

"What is truth?"

John 18:38

I thirst for truth, but shall not reach it until I reach the source.

Robert Browning

Truth and love are wings that cannot be separated, for truth cannot fly without love, nor can love soar aloft without truth.

Ephraem the Syrian

Truth is given, not to be contemplated, but to be done. Life is an action, not a thought.

Frederick William Robertson

O love that passeth knowledge,
T hee I need;
Pour in the heavenly sunshine;
Fill my heart;
Scatter the cloud, the doubting, and the dread,
The joy unspeakable to me impart.

Horatius Bonar

But when he, the Spirit of truth, comes, he will guide you into all the truth.

John 16:13 NIV

For the word of the LORD is right,
And all His work is done in truth.

Psalm 33:4

My prayer is to You,
O LORD, in the acceptable time.

Psalm 69:13

The prayer that begins with trustfulness, and passes on into waiting, will always end in thankfulness, triumph and praise.

Alexander Maclaren

God looks not at the oratory of your prayers, how elegant they may be; nor at the geometry of your prayers, how long they may be; nor at the arithmetic of your prayers, how many they may be; not at the logic of your prayers, how methodical they may be; but the sincerity of them He looks at.

Thomas Brooks

O my divine Master, teach me to hold myself in silence before you, to adore you in the depths of my being, to wait upon you always and never to ask anything of you but the fulfilment of your will.

Teach me to let you act in my soul, and form in it the simple prayer that says little but includes everything. Grant me this favour for the glory of your name.

Jean Nicolas Grou

The soul, like the body, lives by what it feeds on.

Josiah Gilbert Holland

[The people asked:] "Why don't you give us a clue about who you are, just a hint of what's going on? When we see what's up, we'll commit ourselves. Show us what you can do. Moses fed our ancestors with bread in the desert. It says so in the Scriptures: 'He gave them bread from heaven to eat.'"

Jesus responded, "The real significance of that Scripture is not that Moses gave you bread from heaven but that my Father is right now offering you bread from heaven, the real bread. The Bread of God came down out of heaven and is giving life to the world."

They jumped at that: "Master, give us this bread, now and forever!"

Jesus said, "I am the Bread of Life. The person who aligns with me hungers no more and thirsts no more, ever."

John 6:30-35 MSG

Lord, of thy goodness, give me thyself.

Augustine Baker

The soul would have no rainbow had the eyes had no tears.

John Vance Cheney

Life is not a cloudless journey,
Storms and darkness oft oppress,
But the Father's changeless mercy
Comes to cheer the heart's distress;
Heavy clouds may darkly hover,
Hiding all faith's view above,
But across the thickest darkness
Shines the rainbow of His love.

Flora Kirkland

Why should we hang down our heads? Why do we not pluck up good hearts and be of good cheer? God is our father, our best friend, our daily benefactor. Let us, therefore, rejoice and be merry; for heaven is ours, earth is ours, God is ours, Christ is ours, all is ours.

Arthur Dent

Sing to the LORD with thanksgiving;
Sing praises on the harp to our God,
Who covers the heavens with clouds.

Psalm 147:7–8

To you before your passion
They sang their hymns of praise;
To you now high exalted
Our melody we raise.
You accepted their praises;
Accept the prayers we bring
Who in all good delights,
Oh good and gracious King.

Theodulph of Orleans, adapted

The next day a great multitude that had come to the feast, when they heard that Jesus was coming to Jerusalem, took branches of palm trees and went out to meet Him, and cried out: "Hosanna! 'Blessed is He who comes in the name of the Lord!' The King of Israel!"

John 12:12–13

Excitement mounted. An enthusiastic crowd had gathered, some waving branches of palm trees. Others, to show their respect, spread clothes on the road before him. Shouts of praise rang out. The tumultuous, joyous entry of Jesus is described in all four Gospels, signifying just how important this event was.

Just as those men, women and children of long ago welcomed Jesus into their city, we can each welcome him into our lives. When we greet him with the same enthusiasm, love and respect that they showed, we are rewarded with the joy of his presence.

A. M.

'For I will restore health to you and heal you of your wounds,' says the LORD.

Jeremiah 30:17

Look to your health; and if you have it, praise God and value it next to a good conscience; for health is the second blessing that we mortals are capable of—a blessing that money cannot buy; therefore value it, and be thankful for it.

Izaak Walton

Wellness—balance of health of body, mind and soul—is something to work and pray for. The Lord promises restoration of health, healing and safekeeping. Let us do our part so He can do what we cannot.

A. M.

Do you not know that your body is the temple of the Holy Spirit who is in you, whom you have from God, and you are not your own?

1 Corinthians 6:19

Then your light shall break forth like the morning, your healing shall spring forth speedily.

Isaiah 58:8

In the morning you shall see the glory of the Lord.

Exodus 16:7

Every day is a fresh beginning,
    Every morning is the world made new.
Susan Coolidge

Begin at once; before you venture away from this quiet moment, ask your King to take you wholly into His service, and place all the hours of this day quite simply at his disposal, and ask Him to make and keep you ready to do just exactly what He appoints. Never mind about tomorrow; one day at a time is enough.

Try it today, and see if it is not a day of strange, almost curious peace, so sweet that you will be only too thankful, when tomorrow comes, to ask Him to take it also,—till it will become a blessed habit to hold yourself simply and 'wholly at Thy commandment for any manner of service.'
Frances Ridley Havergal

YET I argue not
Against Heaven's hand or will,
    nor bate a jot
Of heart or hope; but still bear up and steer
    Right onward.

J. Milton

If you really fulfill the royal law according to the Scripture, "You shall love your neighbor as yourself," you do well.

James 2:8

Our God-given responsibility to love others is spelled out in the Old Testament,[1] and asserted by Jesus[2] and His followers.[3] Christian authors through the ages have returned repeatedly to the theme. One of these, Betty J. Eadie, expressed our duty beautifully when she wrote:

"Whatever we become here in mortality is meaningless unless it is done for the benefit of others. Our gifts and talents are given to us to help us serve. And in serving others we grow spiritually. We are here to help each other, to care for each other, to understand, forgive and serve one another. We are here to have love for every person on earth."

A. M. [1]*Leviticus 19:18;* [2]*Matthew 22:39;* [3]*Galatians 5:14*

True love ennobles and dignifies the material labors of life; and homely services rendered for love's sake have in them a poetry that is immortal.

Harriet Beecher Stowe

In the morning my prayer comes before You.

Psalm 88:13

Come into my soul, Lord,
As the dawn breaks into the sky;
Let your sun rise in my heart
At the coming of the day.

Traditional

The first hour of the morning is the rudder of the day.

Henry Ward Beecher

I know the morning—I am acquainted with it, and I love it. I love it fresh and sweet as it is—a daily new creation, breaking forth and calling all that have life and breath and being to a new adoration, new enjoyments, and new gratitude.

Daniel Webster

The morning steals upon the night, melting the darkness.

William Shakespeare

He shall be like the light of the morning
when the sun rises,
A morning without clouds,
Like the tender grass
springing out of the earth,
By clear shining after rain.

2 Samuel 23:4

The nail-pierced hands of Jesus reveal the love-filled heart of God.

Author unknown

He poured out His soul unto death...
And He bore the sin of many.

Isaiah 53:12

A man who was completely innocent offered himself as a sacrifice for the good of others, including his enemies, and became the ransom of the world. It was a perfect act.

Mahatma Gandhi

God so loved the world that He gave His only begotten Son, that whoever believes in Him should not perish but have everlasting life.

John 3:16

Eternal light, shine into our hearts,
Eternal goodness, deliver us from evil,
Eternal power, be our support,
Eternal wisdom,
    scatter the darkness of our ignorance,
Eternal pity, have mercy upon us;
That with all our heart and mind
    and soul and strength
We may seek thy face
And be brought by thine infinite mercy
    to thy holy presence;
Through Jesus Christ our Lord.

Alcuin of York

I am He who lives, and was dead, and behold, I am alive forevermore.

Revelation 1:18

"He is not here; for He is risen," we are told.[1] We stand amazed, just as those early witnesses. How could a lifeless, broken body, laying in the cold and dark of the tomb, spring to life? The miracle of Christ's resurrection, flouting the natural order, is truly beyond our human comprehension.

Yet the miracle doesn't end there, as C. S. Lewis wrote, "Jesus has forced open a door that had been locked since the death of the first man. He has met, fought, and beaten the King of Death. Everything is different because he has done so." His resurrection gives us hope for our own. The unknown person who stated, "The best news the world ever had came from a graveyard" sums it up so well.

A. M.   [1]*Matthew 28:6*

Christ has triumphed, and we conquer
By His mighty enterprise,
We with Him to life eternal
By His resurrection rise.

Christopher Wordsworth

I go and prepare a place for you, that where I am, there you may be also.

John 14:3

Brief life is here our portion;
Brief sorrow, short-lived care;
The life that knows no ending,
The tearless life, is there.

There grief is turned to pleasure;
Such pleasure as below
No human voice can utter,
No human heart can know.

And after fleshly weakness,
And after this world's night,
And after storm and whirlwind,
Are calm, and joy, and light.

And He, whom now we trust in,
Shall then be seen and known;
And they that know and see Him
Shall have Him for their own.

The morning shall awaken,
The shadows flee away,
And each true hearted servant
Shall shine as doth the day.

There God, our King and Portion,
In fullness of His grace,
We then shall see forever,
And worship face to face.

St Bernard of Morlaix, translated by John M. Neale

The Lord is your keeper;

The Lord is your shade at your right hand.
The sun shall not strike you by day,
Nor the moon by night.
The Lord shall preserve you from all evil;
He shall preserve your soul.
The Lord shall preserve your going out
    and your coming in
From this time forth, and even forevermore.

Psalm 121:5–8

Blessed trust! That can thus confidingly say, "This hour is mine with its present duty; the next is God's and when it comes, His presence will come with it."

Author unknown

O Christ, the keeper of us all, let thy right hand guard and protect me day and night, when I rest at home, when I walk in my work abroad, when I lie down and when I rise up, that I may not anywhere fail. I commit my whole being unto thee; take charge of me; provide for all my real needs, from this moment forth and always.

Nerses

I will praise You, for I am fearfully and wonderfully made.

Psalm 139:14

I am not what I might be, I am not what I ought to be, I am not what I wish to be, I am not what I hope to be; but I thank God I am not what I once was, and I can say with the great apostle, "By the grace of God I am what I am."

John Newton

Commit yourself to a dream. Nobody who tries to do something great but fails is a total failure. Why? Because he can always rest assured that he succeeded in life's most important battle—he defeated the fear of trying.

Robert H. Schuller

There is a great deal of unmapped country within us.

George Elliot

Short is the little time which remains to thee of life. Live as on a mountain.

Marcus Aurelius Antoninus

Happy is he who makes daily progress and who considers not what he did yesterday but what advance he can make today.

Jerome

Do not hide Your face from me
in the day of my trouble;

Incline Your ear to me;
In the day that I call, answer me speedily.

Psalm 102:2

"All the paths of the Lord are loving and faithful."[1] I have pondered this verse lately, and have found that it feeds my spirit. All does not mean "all—except the paths I am walking in now," or "nearly all—except this especially difficult and painful path." All must mean all.

So, your path with its unexplained sorrow or turmoil, and mine with its sharp flints and briers—and both our paths, with their unexplained perplexity, their sheer mystery— they are His paths, on which He will show himself loving and faithful. Nothing else; nothing less.

Amy Carmichael. [1]*Psalm 25:10*

I will lift up my eyes to the hills—
From whence comes my help?
My help comes from the Lord,
Who made heaven and earth.

Psalm 121:1–2

Now is the watchword of the wise.

Charles Haddon Spurgeon

There is a time to be born, and a time to die, says Solomon,[1] and it is the memento of a truly wise man; but there is an interval between these two times of infinite importance.

Leigh Richmond. [1]*Ecclesiastes 3:2*

There is not a single moment in life that we can afford to lose.

Edward M. Goulburn

What is not started today is never finished tomorrow.

Johann Wolfgang von Goethe

The first step towards getting somewhere is to decide that you are not going to stay where you are.

Chauncey Depew

The vision must be followed by the venture. It is not enough to stare up the steps; we must step up the stairs.

Vance Havner

Time is not a commodity that can be stored for future use. It must be invested hour by hour, or else it is gone forever.

Thomas Alva Edison

Let us love

If you love those who love you, what reward have you? Do not even the tax collectors do the same? And if you greet your brethren only, what do you do more than others?

Matthew 5:46–47

Love is greater than faith, because the end is greater than the means. What is the use of having faith? It is to connect the soul with God. And what is the object of connecting man with God? That he may become like God. But God is Love. Hence Faith, the means, is in order to Love, the end. Love, therefore, obviously is greater than faith. "If I have all faith, so as to remove mountains, but have not love, I am nothing."[1]

Henry Drummond. [1] Corinthians 13:2 (ASV)

He that sows, even with tears, the precious seed of faith, hope and love, shall doubtless come again with joy, bringing his sheaves with him,[1] because it is the very nature of that seed to yield a joyful harvest.

Richard Cecil. [1] Psalm 126:6

I have a home

In My Father's house are many mansions; if it were not so, I would have told you. I go to prepare a place for you. And if I go and prepare a place for you, I will come again and receive you to Myself; that where I am, there you may be also.

John 14:2–3

Eternity is the divine treasure house, and hope is the window, by means of which mortals are permitted to see, as through a glass dearly, the things which God is preparing.

William Mountford

Our home, our country, is heaven, where there are no sorrows, nor fears, nor troubles: this world is the place of our travel and pilgrimage, and, at the best, our inn.

Matthew Hale

I have a home, forever free
From toil, and care, and misery,
Where stormy seas can never roll,
Where bliss eternal crowns the soul.

I have a home prepared for me,
A mansion bright across the sea;
And when I pass to yon bright shore,
I'll dwell with Christ forevermore.

Barney E. Warren

A righteous man may fall seven times
And rise again.

Proverbs 24:16

Great faith is not the faith that walks always in the light and knows no darkness, but the faith that perseveres in spite of God's seeming silences, and that faith will most certainly and surely get its reward.

Father Andrew

'Tis easy enough to be pleasant,
When life flows along like a song,
But the man worthwhile
Is the one who will smile
When everything goes dead wrong.

Ella Wheeler Wilcox

You have set yourselves a difficult task, but you will succeed if you persevere; and you will find a joy in overcoming obstacles. Remember, no effort that we make to attain something beautiful is ever lost.

Helen Keller

My grace is sufficient for you, for My strength is made perfect in weakness.

2 Corinthians 12:9

The people walking in darkness
have seen a great light;

on those living in the land of deep darkness
a light has dawned.

Isaiah 9:2 NIV

Dear Jesus,

You are the joy and the rejoicing of my heart, the sunshine of my soul, the light of my life. Thank you for reaching into the depths of my soul, opening the windows of heaven upon my life and causing your light to burst forth. Like the blind man to whom you brought sight so long ago, sometimes I have felt as though I am living in darkness, but then you thrust me into the world of seeing, a world of light.

I want to keep that thrill of soul and not allow the cares of this life—the burdens, the trials, the heartaches—to eclipse the marvellous light that you have shed abroad in my heart. I want to always keep my eyes on you, so that your power of love can shine brighter and brighter in me, while the things of the world grow dimmer and dimmer. You are the light and love of my life.

No man can do a greater honour to God than to count him true.

Patrick Hamilton

Do you have faith? Have it to yourself before God.

Romans 14:22

Understanding is the reward of faith. Therefore, do not seek to understand in order to believe, but believe that you may understand.

Augustine of Hippo

Faith tells us of things we have never seen, and cannot come to know by our natural senses.

John of the Cross

Faith is a grand cathedral, with divinely pictured windows. Standing without, you can see no glory, nor can imagine any, but standing within every ray of light reveals a harmony of unspeakable splendours.

Nathaniel Hawthorne

Corrie ten Boom survived a concentration camp and the death of her closest family during the Second World War. She went on to share her faith with the world, telling us, "Faith sees the invisible, believes the unbelievable and receives the impossible."

Now may the Lord direct your hearts into the love of God and into the patience of Christ.

2 Thessalonians 3:5

The life of faith is the revelation of Jesus to the soul; the inshining of the glorious gospel; his indwelling and illuminating presence, rooting and grounding us in love. ... Belief without the abiding presence of Jesus pines and dies, but the abiding presence keeps faith alive.

Robert Milman

Long did I toil, and knew no earthly rest,
Far did I rove, and found no certain home;
At last I sought them
   in his sheltering breast,
Who opens his arms,
   and bids the weary come.
With him I found a home, a rest divine,
And I since then am his, and he is mine.

John Quarles

But God showed his great love for us by sending Christ to die for us while we were still sinners.

Romans 5:8 NLT

Then a voice came from the throne [in heaven], saying, "Praise our God, all you His servants and those who fear Him, both small and great!"

Revelation 19:5

Enjoy the blessings of this day, as God sends them; and the difficulties of it bear patiently and sweetly; for this day is only ours, we are dead to yesterday, and we are not yet born to the morrow.

Jeremy Taylor

Do not spoil what you have by desiring what you have not; remember that what you now have was once among the things you only hoped for.

Epicurus

We tend to forget that happiness doesn't come as a result of getting something we don't have, but rather of recognising and appreciating what we do have.

Fredrich Gottlob Koenig

Happiness is like manna; it is to be gathered in grains, and enjoyed every day. It will not keep; it cannot be accumulated; ... it has rained down from heaven, at our very doors.

Tryon Edwards

His banner over me was love.

Song of Solomon 2:4

Come home, my soul, my wandering, tired, grieved soul! Love where thy love shall not be lost. Love him that will not reject thee, nor deceive thee, nor requite thee with injuries as the world does. The peaceable region is above. Retire to the harbour if you would be free from storms. God will receive you when the world does cast you off.

Richard Baxter

Rock of Ages, cleft for me,
Let me hide myself in Thee;
Let the water and the blood,
From Thy wounded side which flowed,
Be of sin the double cure,
Save from wrath and make me pure.

Augustus M. Toplady

I love the LORD, because He has heard
My voice and my supplications.

Psalm 116:1

In Your light we see light.

Psalm 36:9

What do we know of light? By refraction and reflection we learn more of the nature and beauty of light; we can analyse and we can feel. Look at those rosy tints on the snow-clad mountain, that wonderful glow in the western sky, those gorgeous clouds; see the rays of the setting sun lighting up some beautiful old ruin. Is there not something here which reveals to us more of a wonderful beauty and harmony than light alone unmingled with these forms of matter?

Well, hereafter, not on mountain, and sky, and ruin, but on the glistering robes of a great multitude, we shall see reflected the glory of God himself. By the light he gives we shall see the light which he is.

Rev Canon Money, adapted

God said, "Let there be light"; and there was light.

And God saw the light, that it was good; and God divided the light from the darkness.

Genesis 1:3–4

Christ in you, the hope of glory.

Colossians 1:27

Being a Christian is more than just an instantaneous conversion—it is a daily process whereby you grow to be more and more like Christ.

William Franklin (Billy) Graham

The secret of a Christian is that the supernatural is made natural in him by the grace of God, and the experience of this works out in the practical details of life.

Oswald Chambers

To be like Christ. That is our goal, plain and simple. It sounds like a simple, relaxing, easy objective. But stop and think. He learned obedience by the things he suffered. So must we. It is neither easy nor quick nor natural. It is impossible in the flesh, slow in coming, and supernatural in scope. Only Christ can accomplish it within us.

Charles R. Swindoll

That energy is God's energy, an energy deep within you, God himself willing and working.

Philippians 2:13 MSG

Flood my soul and let me shine

For it is the God who commanded light to shine out of darkness, who has shone in our hearts to give the light of the knowledge of the glory of God in the face of Jesus Christ.

2 Corinthians 4:6

Dear Lord,

Help me to spread your fragrance wherever I go. Flood my soul with your spirit and life. Penetrate and possess my whole being so utterly that all my life may only be a radiance of yours. Shine through me, and be so in me that every soul I come in contact with may feel your presence in my soul.

Let them look up and see no longer me, but only you, O Lord! Stay with me and then I will begin to shine as you do; so to shine as to be a light to others. The light, O Lord, will be all from you; none of it will be mine. It will be you shining on others through me.

Let me thus praise you in the way that you love best, by shining on those around me.

John Henry Newman

Prayer is not overcoming God's reluctance; it is laying hold of His highest willingness.

Richard Chenevix Trench

This is the confidence that we have in Him, that if we ask anything according to His will, He hears us. And if we know that He hears us, whatever we ask, we know that we have the petitions that we have asked of Him.

1 John 5:14–15

Wonder at the love of God! He receives our prayers as if they were things of value. He longs that we should love him; and He receives our petitions for blessings as favours done to himself. He has greater joy in giving than we in receiving.

Gregory of Nazianzus

Our prayers and God's mercy are like two buckets in a well; while the one ascends, the other descends.

Mark Hopkins

Most assuredly, I say to you, whatever you ask the Father in My name He will give you.

John 16:23

The centre

God anointed Jesus of Nazareth with the Holy Spirit and with power, who went about doing good and healing all who were oppressed by the devil, for God was with Him.

Acts 10:38

Jesus had no servants,
   yet they called Him Master.
He had no medicines,
   yet they called Him Healer.
He had no army,
   yet kings feared Him.
He won no military battles,
   yet He conquered the world.
He committed no crime,
   yet they crucified Him.
He was buried in a tomb,
   yet He lives today.

Author unknown

Jesus Christ is the centre of all, and the goal to which all tends.

Blaise Pascal

Having been perfected, He [Jesus] became the author of eternal salvation to all who obey Him.

Hebrews 5:9

Our labour here is brief,
but the reward is eternal.

Clare of Assisi

Man goes out to his work and to his labour until the evening. Whatever your hand finds to do, do it with your might. When you eat the labour of your hands, you shall be happy, and it shall be well with you. That every man should eat and drink and enjoy the good of all his labour ... is the gift of God.

Based on Psalm 104:23, 128:2; Ecclesiastes 9:10, 3:13

He who labours as he prays lifts up his heart to God with his hands.

St Bernard of Clairvaux

Lord, in union with your love, unite my work with your great work, and perfect it. As a drop of water, poured into a river, is taken up into the activity of the river, so may my labour become part of your work. Thus may those among whom I live and work be drawn into your love.

Gertrude the Great

The grass withers, the flower fades,
But the word of our God stands forever.

Isaiah 40:8

We must make a great difference between God's word and the word of man. A man's word is a little sound, that flies into the air and soon vanishes; but the word of God is greater than heaven and earth, yea, greater than death and hell, for it forms part of the power of God and endures everlastingly.

Martin Luther

Many books in my library are now behind and beneath me. They were good in their way once, and so were the clothes I wore when I was ten years old; but I have outgrown them. Nobody ever outgrows Scripture; the book widens and deepens with our years.

Charles Haddon Spurgeon

Faith comes by hearing, and hearing by the word of God.

Romans 10:17

God is the beyond in the midst of life.

Dietrich Bonhoeffer

Can anything ever separate us from Christ's love? Does it mean he no longer loves us if we have trouble or calamity, or are persecuted, or hungry, or destitute, or in danger, or threatened with death? No, despite all these things, overwhelming victory is ours through Christ, who loved us.

Romans 8:35–37 NLT

To nestle in front of a fire on a freezing winter's evening, cosy in the folds of a warm blanket, is a picture of momentary comfort; to know we are loved is even more comforting. Let us be reassured of this fact in the words of author John Ortberg: "Nothing you will ever do could make God love you more than he does right now: not greater achievement, not greater beauty, not wider recognition, not even greater levels of spirituality and obedience. Nothing you have ever done could make God love you any less: not any sin, not any failure, not any guilt, not any regret."

A. M.

Safe in the arms of Jesus,
Safe on His gentle breast.
Here no fears alarm me,
Here can my soul find rest.

Fanny Crosby

This is the day the Lord has made;
We will rejoice and be glad in it.

Psalm 118:24

An old man who had lived buoyantly through eighty years was asked, "Which is the happiest season of life?" He replied thoughtfully:

"When spring comes, the air is soft, the buds are breaking on the trees and they are covered with blossoms. I think, how beautiful is spring!

"And when the summer comes, and covers the trees and bushes with heavy foliage, and singing birds mingle with branches, I think, how beautiful is summer!

"When autumn loads them with golden fruit, and their leaves bear the gorgeous tint of frost, I think, how beautiful is autumn!

"And when it is sore winter, and there is neither foliage nor fruit, then when I look up through the leafless branches and see, as I can see in no other season, the shining stars of heaven, I think, how beautiful is the winter of life!"

Adapted

Cheerfulness is a friend to grace; it puts the heart in tune to praise God.

Thomas Watson

Sweet hour of prayer

In the morning, having risen a long while before daylight, He went out and departed to a solitary place; and there He prayed.

Mark 1:35

Sweet hour of prayer! Sweet hour of prayer!
Thy wings shall my petition bear
To Him whose truth and faithfulness
Engage the waiting soul to bless.

And since He bids me seek His face,
Believe His Word and trust His grace,
I'll cast on Him my every care,
And wait for thee, sweet hour of prayer!

William W. Walford

O God, who art peace everlasting, whose chosen reward is the gift of peace, and who has taught us that the peacemakers are thy children, pour thy sweet peace into our souls, that everything discordant may utterly vanish, and all that makes for peace be sweet to us forever. Amen.

Gelasian Sacramentary

On the other side

Jesus made His disciples get into the boat and go before Him to the other side. Now when evening came, He was alone there. But the boat was now in the middle of the sea, tossed by the waves, for the wind was contrary.

Now in the fourth watch of the night Jesus went to them, walking on the sea. And when the disciples saw Him walking on the sea, they were troubled, saying, "It is a ghost!" And they cried out for fear.

But immediately Jesus spoke to them, saying, "Be of good cheer! It is I; do not be afraid." Peter said, "Lord, if it is You, command me to come to You on the water." So Jesus said, "Come."

And when Peter had come down out of the boat, he walked on the water to go to Jesus. But when he saw that the wind was boisterous, he was afraid; and beginning to sink he cried out, saying, "Lord, save me!" And immediately Jesus stretched out His hand and caught him, and said to him, "O you of little faith, why did you doubt?"

Matthew 14:22–31, abridged

Peter learned, and quickly forgot, the lesson of looking to Jesus.[1] If we want to pass safely over our own sea of troubles, we should remember to keep our eyes on the Author and Finisher of our faith.

[1]Hebrews 12:2

Where can I go from Your Spirit?

Or where can I flee from Your presence?
If I ascend into heaven, You are there;
If I make my bed in hell, behold, You are there.
If I take the wings of the morning,
And dwell in the uttermost parts of the sea,
Even there Your hand shall lead me,
And Your right hand shall hold me.

Psalm 139:7–10

Thank you, Lord, for always being with me, no matter whether I am trudging through the valley of sorrow, or strolling through meadows of joy; surviving in the desert of need, or swimming in the oceans of plenty; climbing the mountain of difficulty, or resting in an oasis of peace. No matter my circumstances, you are always constant, and for that I give you my heartfelt thanks.

A generous person will prosper; whoever refreshes others will be refreshed.

Proverbs 11:25 NIV

To the world you are just one person, but to one person you could mean the world.

Author unknown

You must give some time to your fellow men. Even if it's a little thing, do something for others—something for which you get no pay but the privilege of doing it.

Albert Schweitzer

If only we could realize while we are yet mortals that day by day we are building for eternity, how different our lives in many ways would be! Every gentle word, every generous thought, every unselfish deed will become a pillar of eternal beauty in the life to come. We cannot be selfish and unloving in one life and generous and loving in the next. The two lives are too closely blended—one but a continuation of the other.

Rebecca Springer

A generous man devises generous things,
And by generosity he shall stand.

Isaiah 32:8

The love of Christ which passes knowledge

[I would that you] may be able to comprehend what is the width and length and depth and height—to know the love of Christ which passes knowledge; that you may be filled with all the fullness of God.

Ephesians 3:18–19

Sweet Jesus, who shall lend me wings
Of peace and perfect love,
That I may rise from earthly things
To rest with thee above?

Author unknown

Without Christ you are like a sheep without its shepherd; like a tree without water at its roots; like a mere leaf in the tempest—not bound to the tree of life. With your whole heart seek him, and he will be found of you: only give yourself thoroughly up to the search, and truly, you will yet discover him to your joy and gladness.

Charles Haddon Spurgeon, adapted

The steps of faith fall on the seeming void, but find the rock beneath.

John Greenleaf Whittier

Faith is the substance of things hoped for, the evidence of things not seen.

Hebrews 11:1

Live in faith and hope, though it be in darkness, for in this darkness God protects the soul. Cast your care upon God, for you are his and he will not forget you.

John of the Cross

Never let go of hope. One day you will see that it all has finally come together. What you have always wished for has finally come to be. You will look back and laugh at what has passed and you will ask yourself, *How did I get through all of that?*

Author unknown

For who is God, except the LORD?
And who is a rock, except our God?
The LORD lives!
Blessed be my Rock!
Let God be exalted,
The Rock of my salvation!

2 Samuel 22:32,47

When He had called all the multitude to Himself, He said to them, "Hear Me, everyone, and understand."

Mark 7:14

It is the man of prayer that receives large communications from God.

James Harrington Evans

Not in the earthquake or devouring flame,
But in the hush
   that could all fear transform,
The still, small whisper
   to the prophet came.

Oh soul, keep silence on the mount of God!
Though cares and needs
   throb around like a sea
From supplication and desires unshod,
Be still and hear what God shall say to thee.

Mary Rowles Jarvis

The best and sweetest flowers in paradise, God gives to His people when they are on their knees in the closet. Prayer, if not the very gate of heaven, is the key to let us into its ... joys.

Thomas Brooks

Lilies of the field

Consider the lilies of the field, how they grow: they neither toil nor spin; and yet I say to you that even Solomon in all his glory was not arrayed like one of these. Now if God so clothes the grass of the field, which today is, and tomorrow is thrown into the oven, will He not much more clothe you?

Matthew 6:28–30

"Consider the lilies," Jesus tells us. As we think of all the wonder and beauty of the flowers, the anxious spirit that haunts and distresses us often will be put to shame. We learn to trust the wisdom, love and power of him who clothes the little blossoms. The future may look dark, but that flower in the foreground takes away its awe.

Canon Wynne

With grateful hearts the past we own;
The future, all to us unknown,
We to thy guardian care commit,
And peaceful leave before thy feet.

Philip Doddridge

The beginning and the end

I heard a loud voice from heaven saying, "Behold, the tabernacle of God is with men, and He will dwell with them, and they shall be His people. God Himself will be with them and be their God."

Revelation 21:3

Every natural longing has its natural satisfaction. If we thirst, God has created liquids to gratify thirst. If we thirst for life and love eternal, it is likely that there are an eternal life and an eternal love to satisfy that craving.

Frederick William Robertson, adapted

We are born for a higher destiny than that of earth.—There is a realm where the rainbow never fades, where the stars will be spread out before us like islands that slumber on the ocean, and where the beings that pass before us like shadows will stay in our presence forever.

Edward Bulwer-Lytton

As it is written:
"Eye has not seen, nor ear heard,
Nor have entered into the heart of man
The things which God has prepared for those who love Him."

1 Corinthians 2:9

Thou art my God, and I will praise thee:
Thou art my God, I will exalt thee.

Psalm 118:28 KJV

Give me thy grace, good Lord,
To set the world at nought;
To set my mind fast upon thee,
And not to hang upon the blast
    of men's mouths;
To be content to be solitary;
Not to long for worldly company;
To lean unto the comfort of God;
Busily to labour to love him;
To humble and meeken myself
Under the mighty hand of God.

Thomas More

Open to me the gates of righteousness:
I will go into them,
    and I will praise the LORD:
I will praise thee: for thou hast heard me,
    and art become my salvation.

Psalm 118:19,21 KJV

They broke bread in their homes and ate together with glad and sincere hearts.

Acts 2:46

Home is where the heart is.

Pliny the Elder

Most people have forgotten nowadays what a home can mean, though some of us have come to realise it as never before. It is a kingdom of its own in the midst of the world, a haven of refuge amid the turmoil of our age, nay more, a sanctuary. It is not founded on the shifting sands of private and public life, but has its peace in God. For it is God who gave it its special meaning and dignity, its nature and privilege, its destiny and worth.

Dietrich Bonhoeffer

But every house where Love abides,
And Friendship is a guest,
Is surely home, and home-sweet-home:
For there the heart can rest.

Henry Van Dyke

My people will live in a peaceful habitation, in safe dwellings, and in quiet resting places.

Isaiah 32:18 WEB

**Give ear to my words, O LORD,
Consider my meditation.**

Psalm 5:1

As the sun radiates, the day illuminates, the fountain irrigates, the shower sprinkles of its own accord spontaneously, so the spirit of God infuses itself into us. When the soul, gazing heavenward, has come to know its Maker, it is exalted far above all earthly principality and power, and begins already to be what it believes itself to be. There can be no poverty when the wealth of heaven has once satiated our heart. We speak with God and God with us. He instructs us. The house that he enriches, none can impoverish.

Robert Milman, adapted

By meditation I can converse with God, solace myself in the arms of the Saviour, bathe myself in the rivers of divine pleasure, tread the paths of my rest, and view the mansions of eternity.

Author unknown

He satisfies the longing soul,
And fills the hungry soul with goodness.

Psalm 107:9

**Behold, I will bring it health and healing;
I will heal them and reveal to them the
abundance of peace and truth.**

Jeremiah 33:6

Isolated from infancy due to being deaf and
blind, after much effort Helen Keller learned to
communicate and went on to achieve a place of
influence in the world. Aptly she tells us,
"Character cannot be developed in ease and
quiet. Only through experience of trial and
suffering can the soul be strengthened,
ambition inspired, and success achieved."

A. M.

May you have enough happiness
    to keep you sweet,
Trials to keep you strong,
    sorrow to keep you human;
Hope to keep you happy,
    failure to keep you humble;
Success to keep you eager,
    friends to give you comfort,
Wealth to meet your needs,
    enthusiasm to look forward;
Faith to banish depression,
And determination enough
    to make each day
        better than yesterday.

Author unknown

God our Savior showed us
how good and kind he is.

Titus 3:4 (CEV)

Dost thou not know that thy God loves thee in the midst of all this? Mountains, when in darkness hidden, are as real as in day, and God's love is as true to thee now as it was in thy brightest moments.

Charles Haddon Spurgeon

We may not climb the heavenly steeps
 To bring the Lord Christ down;
In vain we search the lowest deeps,
 For him no depths can drown;
But warm, sweet, tender, even yet
 A present help is he;
And faith has still its Olivet,
 And love its Galilee.

John Greenleaf Whittier

Go home to your friends, and tell them what great things the Lord has done for you, and how He has had compassion on you.

Mark 5:19

Flowers are lovely;
Love is flower-like;
Friendship is a sheltering tree.

Samuel Taylor Coleridge

Faith, like light, shall always be simple, and unbending; while love, like warmth, should beam forth on every side, and bend to every necessity of our brethren.

Martin Luther

Love suffers long and is kind; love does not envy; love does not parade itself, is not puffed up; does not behave rudely, does not seek its own, is not provoked, thinks no evil; does not rejoice in iniquity, but rejoices in the truth; bears all things, believes all things, hopes all things, endures all things. Love never fails.

1 Corinthians 13:4–8

Life is short. Be swift to love! Make haste to be kind!

Henri-Frédéric Amiel

Peace comes not from the absence of trouble, but from the presence of God.

Author unknown

The triumph of quietness is not ease. It is not absence of disturbing force. It is a triumph over all. In Christ there is the image of this quietness. Galilee's lake in its stillest hour was never so restful as the heart of Jesus. This is the face we want to see. "When he was reviled, he reviled not again."[1] It is *this* quietness that has touched the world's deepest heart.

It is true of our Saviour that he did possess a rest, a peace, a joy, such as the sons of earth and time have never known, and having manifested these on earth, he left us as his own dying legacy, what he calls "my joy," "my peace." In seeking him, we partake of this peace.

William M. Statham, adapted. [1] Peter 2:23 KJV

Be of good courage,
And He shall strengthen your heart,
All you who hope in the LORD.

Psalm 31:24

When He gives quietness,
who then can make trouble?

Job 34:29

How unutterably sweet is the knowledge that our heavenly Father knows us completely. No talebearer can inform on us, no enemy can make an accusation stick; no forgotten skeleton can come tumbling out of our past; no unsuspected weakness in our characters can come to light to turn God away from us, since he knew us utterly before we knew him and called us to himself in the full knowledge of everything that was against us.

Aiden Wilson Tozer

Now, most people would not be willing to die for an upright person, though someone might perhaps be willing to die for a person who is especially good. But God showed his great love for us by sending Christ to die for us while we were still sinners. And since we have been made right in God's sight by the blood of Christ, he will certainly save us from God's condemnation.

Romans 5:7–9 NLT

Doubt is not the opposite of faith; it is one element of faith.

Paul Tillich

Jesus said to him, "If you can believe, all things are possible to him who believes."

Immediately the father of the child cried out and said with tears, "Lord, I believe; help my unbelief!"

Mark 9:23–24

Thou, to whom all are known
From the cradle to the grave –
   Save, oh! Save.
From doubt, where all is double;
Where wise men are not strong,
Where comfort turns to trouble,
Where just men suffer wrong;
Where sorrow treads on joy,
Where sweet things soonest cloy,
Where faiths are built on dust,
Where love is half mistrust,
Hungry, and barren, and sharp as the sea –
   Oh! Set us free.

Matthew Arnold

Do not fear, for from the first day that you set your heart to understand, and to humble yourself before your God, your words were heard.

Daniel 10:12

Let there be for every pulse a thanksgiving, and for every breath a song.

Johann Wolfgang von Goethe

Imagine a small child with a birthday present. Excitedly he or she tears off the wrapping paper to discover what is in the package. Eyes widen as the new toy is revealed, and there is a shriek of joy. Perhaps the child hugs the doll with golden hair, or starts racing around the room pushing the little car.

That's a tiny picture of the sense of wonder and appreciation we read in the Psalms—so let us express our own wonder and appreciation for all God's gifts.

A. M.

We give thanks to You, O God, we give thanks!
For Your wondrous works
   declare that Your name is near.
For You are great, and do wondrous things;
   You alone are God.
So I will go about Your altar, O LORD,
That I may proclaim
   with the voice of thanksgiving,
And tell of all Your wondrous works.

Psalm 75:1; 86:10; 26:6–7

His face shone like the sun, and His clothes became as white as the light.

Matthew 17:2

Peter was awestruck. He'd trudged up the mountain following Jesus, with James and John at his side. Suddenly Jesus started glowing, and before long, Moses and Elijah—dead for many centuries—appeared and started talking with him.

Peter, the outspoken and sometimes impulsive follower of Jesus, was a man of action. Not content to quietly listen to the amazing conversation in front of him, or even to reflect on its meaning, he interrupted them boldly to suggest:

"Master, this is a great moment! What would you think if I built three memorials here on the mountain—one for you, one for Moses, one for Elijah?"

The conversation came to an abrupt end. God spoke from the cloud, the disciples were petrified and fell flat on their faces, Jesus assuaged their fears, but when they opened their eyes, Moses and Elijah were gone.

Peter had tried to capture the moment, but in so doing, it could be argued that he missed it.

Based on Matthew 17:1-8

Dear Lord, this is the day which You have made. Help me to live in each moment, treasuring the joy that is now. Amen.

Who errs and mends,
to God himself commends.

Miguel de Cervantes

Come back to God, your God, and obey him with your whole heart and soul. ... God, your God, will restore everything you lost; he'll have compassion on you; he'll come back and pick up the pieces from all the places where you were scattered.

Deuteronomy 30:2–3 The Message

In the Bible, the word *repent* comes from the Greek *metanoeo* (New Testament) meaning *to turn around,* or the Hebrew word *shuwb* (Old Testament) meaning to *return* or *come back*. If you find yourself on the wrong path, when you turn around and start heading back in the right direction, you are literally repenting. When Jesus said, "Repent, and believe in the gospel,"[1] He wanted people to not only have faith, but to also change what they were doing or how they were living. Belief plus action is what He expects.

[1]*Mark 1:15*

No one was ever saved because his sins were small; no one was ever rejected on account of the greatness of his sins. Where sin abounds, grace shall much more abound.

Archibald Alexander

Heaven and earth will pass away, but My words will by no means pass away.

Luke 21:33

I consider the Gospels to be thoroughly genuine, for in them there is the effective reflection of a sublimity which emanated from the person of Christ, and this is as divine as ever the divine appeared on earth.

Johann Wolfgang von Goethe

You never get to the end of Christ's words. There is something in them always behind. They pass into proverbs, into laws, into doctrines, into consolations; but they never pass away, and, after all the use that is made of them they are still not exhausted.

Arthur P. Stanley

These writings bring back to you the living image of that most holy mind, the very Christ himself speaking, healing, dying, rising, in fact so entirely present, that you would see less of him if you beheld him with your eyes.

Desiderius Erasmus

If anyone loves Me, he will keep My word; and My Father will love him, and We will come to him and make Our home with him.

John 14:23

Guided to my haven

He calms the storm,
So that its waves are still.
Then they are glad because they are quiet;
So He guides them to their desired haven.

Psalm 107:29–30

Gliding o'er life's fitful waters,
Heavy surges sometimes roll;
And we sigh for yonder haven,
For the homeland of the soul.
'Tis the weary pilgrim's homeland,
Where each throbbing care shall cease,
And our longings and our yearnings,
Like a wave, be hushed to peace.

Fanny Crosby

In our heavenly homeland, peace flows as a river; joy springs as a fountain; love is boundless as an ocean. Our Saviour has gained us entrance to this haven of peace; our fears, our tears, our sorrows are erased in his embrace. Our loved ones wait patiently until they may take us into their arms once more. So far, yet so near! Heaven is but a prayer's breath away.

A. M.

Centred on you

Dear Lord,

In the Bible when Jabez called on you, saying, "Oh, that you would bless me indeed, and enlarge my territory, that your hand would be with me, and that you would keep me from evil, that I may not cause pain," you granted him what he requested.[1] Likewise I ask you to grant me my requests. Please be with me this day; help my thoughts to be centred on you, and my actions to be for the benefit of others.

[1] *1 Chronicles 4:10*

God be in my head,
   and in my understanding;
God be in my eyes,
   and in my looking;
God be in my mouth,
   and in my speaking;
God be in my heart,
   and in my thinking;
God be at my end,
   and at my departing.

Attributed to St Patrick

As for me, I will call upon God,
And the LORD shall save me.

Evening and morning and at noon
I will pray, and cry aloud,
And He shall hear my voice.

Psalm 55:16–17

There are times when solitude is better than society, and silence is wiser than speech. We should be better Christians if we were more alone, waiting upon God, and gathering through meditation on his Word spiritual strength for labour in his service. We ought to muse upon the things of God, because we thus get the real nutriment out of them.

Charles Haddon Spurgeon

If you allow yourself to be constantly distracted, your heart will grow hard. Retire to pray when you can and live the rest of your day in love.

François de la Mothe-Fénelon

I have called, and he has answered,
 Ever faithful does he prove!
He has shown me his salvation,
 And a lifetime of his love.

Author unknown

To God, yes to God, I'll sing, make music to God.

Judges 5:3 MSG

God has prepared for Himself one great song of praise throughout eternity, and those who enter the community of God join in this song. It is the song that the "morning stars sang together and all the sons of God shouted for joy" at the creation of the world.[1] It is the victory song of the children of Israel after passing through the Red Sea, the Magnificat of Mary after the annunciation, the song of Paul and Silas in the night of prison, the song of the singers on the sea of glass after their rescue, the "song of Moses the servant of God, and the song of the Lamb."[2] It is the song of the heavenly fellowship.

Dietrich Bonhoeffer. [1] *Job 38:7* [2] *Revelation 15:3*

When your heart is full of Christ, you want to sing.

Charles Haddon Spurgeon

You will show me the path of life;
In Your presence is fullness of joy.

Psalm 16:11

In the secret of His presence
   how my soul delights to hide!
Oh, how precious are the lessons
   which I learn at Jesus' side!
Earthly cares can never vex me,
   neither trials lay me low;
For when Satan comes to tempt me,
   to the secret place I go.

When my soul is faint and thirsty,
   'neath the shadow of His wing
There is cool and pleasant shelter,
   and a fresh and crystal spring;
And my Saviour rests beside me,
   as we hold communion sweet:
If I tried, I could not utter
   what He says when thus we meet.

Would you like to know the sweetness
   of the secret of the Lord?
Go and hide beneath His shadow:
   this shall then be your reward;
And whene'er you leave the silence
   of that happy meeting place,
You must mind and bear the image
   of the Master in your face.

Ellen L. Goreh

In everything give thanks; for this is the will of God in Christ Jesus for you.

1 Thessalonians 5:18

Reflect upon your blessings, of which every man has plenty, not on your past misfortunes, of which all men have some.

Charles Dickens

Though prayer purchases blessings, giving praise keeps the quiet possession of them.

Thomas Fuller

Praise is the best auxiliary to prayer; and he who most bears in mind what has been done for him by God will be most emboldened to ask for fresh gifts from above.

Henry Melville

Raise your heart continually to God, seek his aid and let the foundation stone of your consolation be your happiness in being his. All vexations and annoyances will be comparatively unimportant while you know that you have such a friend, such a stay, such a refuge. May God be ever in your heart.

Francis de Sales

Blessed be the Lord,
Who daily loads us with benefits,
The God of our salvation!

Psalm 68:19

While they watched, He was taken up, and a cloud received Him out of their sight.

Acts 1:9

Because Christ lives I too shall live,
　　oh glorious truth divine,
To think that resurrection life was his
　　and shall be mine.
Because Christ lives I too shall live,
　　I'll leave this lump of clay
And lift my wings to higher heights
　　on resurrection day.
Because Christ lives I too shall live,
　　with him I'll ever be,
Rejoicing that he broke death's chains
　　and set my spirit free.

Author unknown

James S. Stewart is not overstating when he tells us, "God raised up Jesus, not simply to give credence to man's immemorial hopes of life beyond the grave, but to shatter history and remake it by a cosmic, creative event, ushering in a new age and a new dimension of existence."

Blessed [are] the merciful,
for they shall obtain mercy.

Matthew 5:7

Be kind and merciful. Let no one ever come to you without leaving better and happier. Be the living expression of God's kindness—kindness in your face, kindness in your eyes, kindness in your smile, kindness in your warm greeting. In the slums we are the light of God's kindness to the poor.

To children, to the poor, to all who suffer and are lonely, give always a happy smile. Give them not only your care but also your heart. Because of God's goodness and love every moment of our life can be the beginning of great things. Be open, ready to receive and you will find Him everywhere. Every work of love brings a person face to face with God.

Mother Teresa

Hail! Ye small sweet courtesies of life; for smooth do ye make the road of it, like grace and beauty, which beget inclinations to love at first sight; it is ye who open the door and let the stranger in.

Laurence Sterne

Cause me to hear

Cause me to hear Your lovingkindness
   in the morning,
For in You do I trust;
Cause me to know the way
   in which I should walk,
For I lift up my soul to You.

Psalm 143:8

Walk boldly and wisely. There is a hand above that will help you on.

Philip James Bailey

The quieter the mind, the more powerful, the worthier, the deeper, the more telling and more perfect the prayer is.

Meister Eckhart

I can take my telescope and look millions of miles into space; but I can lay my telescope aside, go into my room and shut the door, and while in earnest prayer I see more of heaven and get closer to God than I can when assisted by all the telescopes and material agencies on earth.

Isaac Newton

Speak, LORD, for Your servant hears.

1 Samuel 3:9

Flowers appear on the earth;
the season of singing has come,
the cooing of doves is heard in our land.

Song of Solomon 2:12

For the beauty of the earth,
For the beauty of the skies,
For the love which from our birth
Over and around us lies,
Lord of all, to thee we raise
This our grateful hymn of praise.

For the beauty of each hour
Of the day and of the night,
Hill and vale, and tree and flower,
Sun and moon and stars of light,
Lord of all, to thee we raise
This our grateful hymn of praise.

For each perfect gift of thine,
To our race so freely given,
Graces human and divine,
Flowers of earth and buds of heaven,
Lord of all, to thee we raise
This our grateful hymn of praise.

Francis Pierpoint

Happy is that people

For thus says the High and Lofty One
Who inhabits eternity, whose name is Holy:
"I dwell in the high and holy place,
With him who has a contrite and humble spirit,
To revive the spirit of the humble,
And to revive the heart of the contrite ones."

Isaiah 57:15

Happiness is made up of many things: It is a smile of a child, the golden glows of a sunrise, the warm hug of a loved one, health after sickness. But such happiness is also transitory: A child does not always smile, the sunrise may be overshadowed with dark clouds, a loved one may leave, sickness may not pass. There is another happiness, that is deeper and everlasting, and that is the happiness that comes into your soul when you realise the depth, breadth and height of God's love for you, a love embodied in his Son, Jesus.

To find Jesus is to discover that no matter your weakness, no matter your inabilities, no matter your despair, there is a strength you can draw upon, a hope you can lean upon, a love you can dwell within. Truly, "Happy is that people, whose God is the Lord."[1]

A. M. [1] *Psalm 144:15 KJV*

Give me understanding according to Your word.

Psalm 119:169

It is a great thing, this reading of the Scriptures! For it is not possible ever to exhaust the mind of the Scriptures. It is a well that has no bottom.

St John Chrysostom

Leave not off reading the Bible till you find your hearts warmed. ... Let it not only inform you, but inflame you.

Thomas Watson

We taste thee, O thou living bread,
And long to feast upon thee still;
We think of thee, the fountain-head,
And thirst our souls from thee to fill.
Our restless spirits yearn for thee,
Where'er our changeful lot is cast;
Glad when thy gracious smile we see,
Blest when our faith can hold thee fast.

St. Bernard of Clairvaux

I will give you the treasures of darkness
And hidden riches of secret places,
That you may know that I, the LORD,
Who call you by your name,
Am the God of Israel.

Isaiah 45:3

What men call accident is the doing of God's providence.

Gamaliel Bailey

To everything there is a season,
    A time for every purpose under heaven:
A time to be born,
    And a time to die;
A time to plant,
    And a time to pluck what is planted;
A time to weep,
    And a time to laugh;
A time to mourn,
    And a time to dance;
A time to cast away stones,
    And a time to gather stones;
A time to embrace,
    And a time to refrain from embracing;
A time to gain,
    And a time to lose;
A time to keep,
    And a time to throw away;
A time to tear,
    And a time to sew;
A time to keep silence,
    And a time to speak;
A time to love,
    And a time to hate;
A time of war,
    And a time of peace.

Ecclesiastes 3:1–2,4–8

Our God lovingly looks after all those who seek him.

Ezra 8:22 MSG

Be still awhile from thy own thoughts, searching, seeking, desires, and imaginations, and be stayed in the principle of God in thee, that it may raise thy mind up to God, and stay it upon God; and thou wilt find strength from Him, and find Him to be a God at hand, a present help in the time of trouble and need.

George Fox

Wait patiently, trust humbly, depend only upon, seek solely to a God of Light and Love, of Mercy and Goodness, of Glory and Majesty, ever dwelling in the inmost depth and spirit of your soul.

WM Law

Within Thy circling arms we lie,
    O God! In Thy infinity:
Our souls in quiet shall abide,
    Beset with love on every side.

Author unknown

This is how we know that we live in him and he in us: He has given us of his Spirit.

1 John 4:13 NIV

No duty is more urgent than that of returning thanks.

Ambrose

Then as He entered a certain village, there met Him ten men who were lepers, who stood afar off. And they lifted up their voices and said, "Jesus, Master, have mercy on us!"

So when He saw them, He said to them, "Go, show yourselves to the priests." And so it was that as they went, they were cleansed.

And one of them, when he saw that he was healed, returned, and with a loud voice glorified God, and fell down on his face at His feet, giving Him thanks. And he was a Samaritan.

So Jesus answered and said, "Were there not ten cleansed? But where are the nine? Were there not any found who returned to give glory to God except this foreigner?"

And He said to him, "Arise, go your way. Your faith has made you well."

Luke 17:12–19

Oh, give thanks to the LORD, for He is good!
For His mercy endures forever.

Psalm 106:1

Peace I leave with you, My peace I give to you; not as the world gives do I give to you. Let not your heart be troubled, neither let it be afraid.

John 14:27

From the world's "hot, restless gleam," from its hopes and fears, joys, sorrows, sins and struggles, we turn to personal communion with him who is touched with the feeling of our infirmities and knows our sorrows. Even as the dewy coolness and the soft twilight shades steal over the day, when the summer day melts into the summer evening, so the sense of pain and shame, anxiety, fatigue, and worry of mind all soften into childlike trust and peaceful confidence as we "cast our care upon him who cares for us."[1]

Canon Wynne, adapted. [1] Peter 5:7

To re-create strength, rest.
To re-create mind, repose.
To re-create cheerfulness, hope in God.

Charles Simmons

He who has no vision of eternity will never get a true hold of time.

Thomas Carlyle

While we look not at the things which are seen, but at the things which are not seen: for the things which are seen are temporal; but the things which are not seen are eternal.

2 Corinthians 4:18 KJV

Our duty as Christians is always to keep heaven in our eye and earth under our feet.

Matthew Henry

Holy Spirit of God, visit now this soul of mine, and tarry within it until the eventide. Inspire all my thoughts. Pervade all my imaginations. Suggest all my decisions. Lodge in my soul's most inward citadel, and order all my doings.

Be with me in silence and in my speech, in my haste and in my leisure, in company and in solitude, in the freshness of the morning and the weariness of the evening. Give me grace at all times to rejoice in thy mysterious companionship.

John Baillie

When you pass through the waters,
I will be with you;
And through the rivers,
they shall not overflow you.

Isaiah 43:2

God doesn't open paths for us in advance of our coming. He doesn't promise help before help is needed. He doesn't remove obstacles out of our way before we reach them. Yet when we are on the edge of our need, God's hand is stretched out. Many people forget this and are forever worrying about difficulties that they foresee in the future. They expect that God is going to make the way plain and open before them miles and miles ahead, whereas he has promised to do it only step by step as they may need. You must get to the floodwaters before you can claim the promise.

Author unknown

Why shouldst thou fill today with sorrow
    About tomorrow,
        My heart?
One watches all with care most true,
Doubt not that He will give thee too
        Thy part.

Paul Flemming

Jesus said to him, "You shall love the Lord your God with all your heart, with all your soul, and with all your mind."

Matthew 22:37

It is not happiness I seek,
Its name I hardly dare to speak;
It is not made for man or earth,
And Heaven alone can give it birth.
There is a something sweet and pure,
Through life, through death it may endure;
With steady foot I onward press,
And long to win that Blessedness.

Louisa J. Hall

My God, I love thee above all else and thee I desire as my last end. Always and in all things, with my whole heart and strength I seek thee. If thou give not thyself to me, thou givest nothing; if I find thee not, I find nothing. Grant to me, therefore, most loving God, that I may ever love thee for thyself above all things, and seek thee in all things in this life present, so that at last I may find thee and keep thee for ever in the world to come.

Thomas Bradwardine

The LORD shall endure forever.

Psalm 9:7

Making tea or coffee requires boiling water. When I heat the water, it boils at 100 degrees centigrade. When my great-grandmother heated water for tea, the water boiled at 100 degrees centigrade. When the people of antiquity heated water, whether in Greece or Rome, China or India, the water boiled at 100 degrees centigrade. We can reasonably expect that our grandchildren will also find that water boils at 100 degrees centigrade.

Some things simply don't change. Water boils; God is.

A. M.

Moses said to God, "Indeed, when I come to the [people] and say to them, 'The God of your fathers has sent me to you,' and they say to me, 'What is His name?' what shall I say to them?"

And God said to Moses, "I AM WHO I AM."

Exodus 3:13–14

Be of good courage,
And He shall strengthen your heart.

Psalm 27:14

The other evening I was riding home after a heavy day's work. I felt very weary and depressed, when swiftly and suddenly that text came to me, "My [Jesus'] grace is sufficient for thee."[1]

I said, "I should think it is, Lord," and burst out laughing. It seemed to make unbelief so absurd.

It was as though some little fish, being very thirsty, was troubled about drinking the river dry, and Father Thames said, "Drink away, little fish, my stream is sufficient for thee."

Again, I imagined a man away up yonder, in a lofty mountain, saying to himself, "I breathe so many cubic feet of air every year, I fear I shall exhaust the oxygen in the atmosphere." But the earth might say, "Breathe away, O man, and fill thy lungs.

My atmosphere is sufficient for thee."

Be great believers! Little faith will bring your souls to Heaven, but great faith will bring Heaven to your souls.

H. Spurgeon. [1] *2 Corinthians 12:9 KJV*

If you have faith
as a grain of mustard seed.

Matthew 17:20

Thomas doubted that Jesus had risen to life following his resurrection; it took the actual sight of the Saviour for him to be convinced. Such privileges are rare in the walk of faith. It seems that more often we are expected to believe without seeing, which can be quite a struggle.

Part of the answer lies around us. The flowers that appear in springtime, the trees laden with fruit, and every rich crop of wheat, corn and rice grows from tiny seeds. Buried unseen in the dark earth, nurtured by the warmth of the sun, watered by the rain, the seeds undergo their transformation. In time they stand as full-grown plants.

That all these plants, with their beauty and usefulness, grow from a tiny seed is an illustration of faith. Jesus himself likened faith to a mustard seed. Faith doesn't start as a majestic tree. It just needs to be a tiny seed. Plant it, believe, and it will grow.

A. M.

Jesus said to him, "Thomas, because you have seen Me, you have believed. Blessed are those who have not seen and yet have believed."

John 20:29

He has made everything beautiful in its time.

Ecclesiastes 3:11

Study nature as the countenance of God.

Charles Kingsley

The person who, in living union of the mind and heart, can converse with God through nature, finds in the material forms around him a source of power and happiness inexhaustible, and like the life of angels.

The highest life and glory of humanity is to be alive unto God; and when this grandeur of responsiveness to him, and this power of communion with him is carried, as the habit of the soul, into the forms of nature, then the walls of our world are as the gates of heaven.

George B. Cheever, adapted

There is a signature of wisdom and power impressed on the works of God. ... Not only the splendour of the sun, but the glimmering light of the glow-worm proclaims his glory.

John Newton

Let us love one another, for love is of God.

1 John 4:7

What do we live for, if it is not to make life less difficult to each other?

George Eliot

If, instead of a gem or even a flower, we could cast the gift of a lovely thought into the heart of a friend, that would be giving as the angels give.

George MacDonald

Eternal goodness,

You want me to gaze into you and see that you love me.

You love me freely, and you want me to love and serve my neighbours with the same love, offering them my prayers and my possessions, as far as in me lies.

O God, come to my assistance!

Catherine of Siena

He who is filled with love is filled with God himself.

Augustine of Hippo

[She] also sat at Jesus' feet and heard His word.

Luke 10:39

God only knows the love of God;
Oh that it now were shed abroad
In this poor stony heart;
For love I sigh, for love I pine;
This only portion, Lord, be mine!
Be mine this better part!

Oh that I could for ever sit,
With Mary, at the Master's feet;
Be this my happy choice!
My only care, delight and bliss,
My joy, my heaven on earth be this,
To hear the Bridegroom's voice!

Charles Wesley

Come, O Christ my Light,
   and illumine my darkness.
Come, my Life,
   and revive me from death.
Come, my Physician,
   and heal my wounds.
Come, Flame of Divine Love,
   and burn up the thorns of my sins,
Kindling my heart
   with the flame of your love.
For you alone are my King and my Lord.

Dimitri of Rostov

Praise you, Lord! Praise your name!

I'm going to bless your name, Lord, from now and forever. From the rising of the sun to when it goes down, your name is to be praised.

You are high above all nations, your glory is above the heavens.

Who is like you, oh Lord my God? You dwell on high, yet you look down and pay attention to the things of this earth. You raise me up when I'm down; you lift me up out of the ash heap! You have given me a roof overhead, and much more.

I love you, Lord, because you have heard my voice and my supplications. Because you have inclined your ear to me, therefore I will call upon you as long as I live.

Praise you, Lord!

Based on Psalm 113 and 116:1–2

Thrice blest will all our blessings be,
When we can look through them to Thee;
When each glad heart its tribute pays
Of love and gratitude and praise.

M.J. Cotterill

Do not be afraid, little flock.

Luke 12:32 GNB

Go to your heavenly Father and tell him you are frightened, and he has ways of taking away these fears, for though they may be ridiculous to some, a child's dreads are never too frivolous for the sympathy of a loving father, but he meets them as if there were some great reality in them, and so sets them aside.

Whatsoever then your want, your woe, your grief, hurry away to your great Father's mercy-seat and spread it there, and he will give you comfort; and ever more believe from this night forward that God does pity all them that fear him, and whatever he sees of weakness in their nature and of sorrow in their lot he will help them. So may you find it now and evermore, for Christ's sake.

Charles Haddon Spurgeon

Jesus! The Name that charms our fears
That bids our sorrows cease.

John Wesley

Whenever I am afraid, I will trust in You.

Psalm 56:3

"The LORD is my portion," says my soul, "Therefore I hope in Him!"

Lamentations 3:24

Finally our hope and faith are strong and steady. Then, when that happens, we are able to hold our heads high no matter what happens and know that all is well, for we know how dearly God loves us.

Romans 5:4–5 TLB

Everything that is done in the world is done by hope.

Martin Luther

Union with Jesus Christ is the foundation of our hope.

Jean-Jacques Pictet

O Christ, our Morning Star, splendour of light eternal, shining with the glory of the rainbow, come and waken us from the greyness of our apathy and renew in us your gift of hope.

The Venerable Bede

May the God of hope fill you with all joy and peace as you trust in him, so that you may overflow with hope by the power of the Holy Spirit.

Romans 15:13 NIV

As sure as ever God puts his children in the furnace, he will be in the furnace with them.

Charles Haddon Spurgeon

These three men, Shadrach, Meshach, and Abednego, fell down bound into the midst of the burning fiery furnace.

Then King Nebuchadnezzar was astonished; and he rose in haste and spoke, saying to his counselors, "Did we not cast three men bound into the midst of the fire?" They answered and said to the king, "True, O king."

"Look!" he answered, "I see four men loose, walking in the midst of the fire; and they are not hurt, and the form of the fourth is like the Son of God."

Daniel 3:23–25

Troubles are an inevitable part of the fabric of life. At times we may wonder if God has forgotten us. Perhaps the three young men, captives of a hostile nation, threatened with execution if they would not renounce their faith, wondered the same. Yet they held firm, and the Lord not only did not fail them, but stood with them in the midst of their trouble.

What greater comfort than to realise that God is with us, no matter the heat of our trial.

A. M.

He said to them,
"Come aside by yourselves to a deserted
place and rest a while."

Mark 6:31

Oh for a 'desert place,'
   with only the Master's smile!
Oh for the 'coming apart,'
   with only His 'rest awhile!'

Many are 'coming and going'
   with busy restless feet,
And the soul is hungering now,
   with 'no leisure so much as to eat.'

Well! I will wait in the crowd
   till He shall call me apart,
Till the silence fall which shall waken
   the music of mind and heart;

Patiently wait till He give
   the work of my secret choice,
Blending the song of life
   with the thrill of the Master's voice.

Frances Ridley Havergal

Good Jesus, strength of the weary, rest of the
restless, by the weariness and unrest of your
sacred cross, come to me who am weary that
I may rest in you.

Edward Pusey

It is in giving that we receive, it is in loving that we are loved.

Francis of Assisi

Kind words are the music of the world. They have a power which seems to be beyond natural causes, as though they were some angel's sons which had lost their way and come to earth.

Frederick William Faber

The cure for all the ills and wrongs, the cares, the sorrows and the crimes of humanity, all lie in that one word "love." It is the divine vitality that everywhere produces and restores life. To each and every one of us, it gives the power of working miracles if we will.

Lydia M. Child

The truly generous is the truly wise, and he who loves not others, lives unblest.

Henry Home

Blessed is the influence of one true, loving human soul on another.

George Eliot

Laugh and grow strong.

St. Ignatius

Make me hear joy and gladness.
Create in me a clean heart, O God,
And renew a steadfast spirit within me.
Restore to me the joy of Your salvation,
And uphold me by Your generous Spirit.

Psalm 51:8, 10, 12

For the test of the heart is trouble, and it always comes with years, and the smile that is worth the praises of earth is the smile that shines through tears.

Ella Wheeler Wilcox

Mirth is the sweet wine of human life. It should be offered sparkling with zestful life unto God.

Henry Ward Beecher

My God, the Spring of all my joys,
The Life of my delights,
The Glory of my brightest days,
And Comfort of my nights!
In darkest shades, if He appear,
My dawning is begun,
He is my soul's bright morning star,
And He my rising sun.

Isaac Watts

I cried out to God and he listened to me.

I am in difficulty and I don't know what else to do but seek his help. I've been up all night; I'm so troubled I couldn't sleep. When I started to grumble and complain about my problems, then I got completely overwhelmed. Something to think about. I can't even put my sorrows into words.

Then again, I remember in the past, when things looked so bleak, he pulled me out of it. When I think back really hard and focus on what he has already done in my life, I can remember the ways he has helped me out.

Is he going to leave me this time? Won't he help me again? Won't he be merciful? Have his promises failed? Has he forgotten how to take care of me—or is he too angry this time? Something else to think about.

But I've got to go back to the crux of the matter. I've got to focus on how he has taken care of me and my loved ones all through the years.—And not just us, but so many of his children throughout the centuries. Just thinking about this and putting it into words is lifting me out of the doldrums.

Yes, God is great; he is taking care of things; he'll even do miracles if that's what it takes. He's going to work things out.

Psalm 77:1–14, loosely paraphrased

**In books I converse with men,
in the Bible I converse with God.**

William Romaine

All scripture is given by inspiration of God, and is profitable for doctrine, for reproof, for correction, for instruction in righteousness.

2 Timothy 3:16

After all, the Bible must be its own argument and defence. The power of it can never be proved unless it is felt. The authority of it can never be supported unless it is manifest. The light of it can never be demonstrated unless it shines.

Henry Van Dyke

Teach me, O LORD,
   the way of Your statutes,
And I shall keep it to the end.
Give me understanding,
   and I shall keep Your law;
Indeed, I shall observe it
   with my whole heart.
Make me walk
   in the path of Your commandments,
For I delight in it.

Psalm 119:33–35

Blessed [are] those who hunger and thirst for righteousness, for they shall be filled.

Matthew 5:6

It is obvious that to be in earnest in seeking the truth is an indispensable requisite for finding it.

John Henry Newman

True wisdom is to know what is best worth knowing, and to do what is best worth doing.

Edward Porter Humphrey

The light which we have gained was given to us, not to be ever staring on, but by it to discover onward things more remote from our knowledge.

John Milton

The words of God which you receive by your ear, hold fast in your heart. For the Word of God is the food of the soul.

St Gregory I

The LORD gives wisdom;
From His mouth come
knowledge and understanding.

Proverbs 2:6

Faith that goes forward triumphs.

Author unknown

A teacher took her primary school students to the assembly hall for a lesson with a difference. Standing at the foot of the steps leading up to the stage, she asked, "Is anybody good at jumping?"

Quite a few young hands shot up.

"Well," she continued, "could any of you jump from the floor here up onto the stage?"

No hands went up this time.

"I can," said the teacher, "and I'll show you how." Beginning at the foot of the steps leading up to the stage, she hopped onto the first step. From there she hopped onto the second, and so on until she reached the top.

Many things can only be accomplished little by little, step by step. When a task looks daunting or the way ahead too steep, just take it one step at a time.

Retold

The LORD will guide you continually.

Isaiah 58:11

O God, make us children of quietness, and heirs of peace.

Clement I of Rome

It is good that one should hope and wait quietly for the salvation of the LORD.

In the [reverence] of the LORD there is strong confidence, and His children will have a place of refuge.

Lamentations 3:26; Proverbs 14:26

Precious hiding place,
In the shelter of His love;
Not a doubt or fear,
Since my Lord is near,
And I'm sheltered in His love.

Avis Christiansen

Peace rules the day when Christ rules the mind.

Author unknown

Let the peace of God rule in your hearts; and be thankful.

Colossians 3:15

For you shall go out with joy,
And be led out with peace;
The mountains and the hills
Shall break forth into singing before you,
And all the trees of the field shall clap their hands.

Isaiah 55:12

**Your mercy, O Lord, is in the heavens;
Your faithfulness reaches to the clouds.**

Psalm 36:5

Skies to be perfectly beautiful must not be cloudless. The sunrise owes half its charms to the morning clouds that catch the glory of the coming day. They are the outriders of the king, heralding his grand approach. And when the giant has run his course and must depart, the evening clouds assist him. In purple robes and crimson vestments with silver lining and golden edgings, he bedecks them all.

The moon, too, uses the clouds to good account. The silver queen appears to know that a thin veil becomes her well. Clouds are the river of God that is full of water.

Thomas Spurgeon

Life to be wonderful is not cloudless. An endless blue sky may represent drought; the appearance of clouds a welcome harbinger of needed rain. Rays of hope shine more brilliantly when reflected off the clouds of disappointment. Clouds, as well as sunshine, bring good things.

A. M.

Gratitude, a taste of heaven

To cultivate the sense of the beautiful is one of the most effectual ways of cultivating an appreciation of the divine goodness.

Christian Nestell Bovee

A thankful soul holds consort with the music of heaven. The little birds do not sip one drop of water, but they look up as if they meant to give thanks;—to show us what we should do for every drop of grace.

Thomas Brooks

Gratitude to God makes even a temporal blessing a taste of heaven.

William Romaine

O render thanks to God above,
The Fountain of eternal love,
Whose mercy firm through ages past
Has stood, and shall forever last.

William Knapp

There you shall eat before the LORD your God, and you shall rejoice in all to which you have put your hand, you and your households, in which the LORD your God has blessed you.

Deuteronomy 12:7

Where then is my hope
—who can see any hope for me?

Job 17:15

O Lord, God of my salvation, I have cried out day and night before You.

Psalm 88:1

Dear Jesus, sometimes I feel broken, even shattered, stunned by life's events and challenges. I'm so glad You came into this world to save us.[1] You help me out when I'm stuck in a corner. Sometimes, when I can't figure out where I should be going, you give me advice. You don't push; sometimes you seem to start down a path so I can follow in your steps. Other times, you shine a light, just enough so I can figure things out. I've had some pretty rough times recently, and it was a relief to have your assurance that I'm never going to be left to manage things entirely by myself. Thank you for the hope you personify.

[1]See John 3:16.

We are pressed on every side by troubles, but we are not crushed. We are perplexed, but not driven to despair. [9] We are hunted down, but never abandoned by God. We get knocked down, but we are not destroyed.

2 Corinthians 4:8–9 NLT

Let us be glad and rejoice
and give Him glory.

Revelation 19:7

There are always flowers for those who want to see them.

Henri Matisse

Gratitude is born in hearts that take time to count up past mercies.

Charles Edward Jefferson

We need deliberately to call to mind the joys of our journey. Perhaps we should try to write down the blessings of one day. We might begin; we could never end; there are not pens or paper enough in all the world.

George A. Buttrick

To God who gives our daily bread
A thankful song we raise,
And that he who sends us food
May fill our hearts with praise.

Thomas Tallis

Be filled with the Spirit, speaking to one another in psalms and hymns and spiritual songs, singing and making melody in your heart to the Lord, giving thanks always for all things to God the Father in the name of our Lord Jesus Christ.

Ephesians 5:18–20

Most high, most powerful, good Lord, to you belong praise, glory, honour and all blessing!

Praised be my Lord God with all his creatures, and especially our brother the sun, who brings us the day and brings us the light; fair is he and shines with a great splendour. O Lord, he signifies you.

Praised be my Lord for our sister the moon and for the stars, which he has set clear and lovely in the heavens.

Praised be my Lord for our brother the wind, and for air and cloud, calms and all weather, by which you uphold life in all creatures.

Praised be my Lord for our sister water, who is very serviceable unto us and humble and precious and pure.

Praised be my Lord for our brother fire, through whom you give light in the darkness, and he is bright and pleasant and very mighty and strong.

Praised be my Lord for our mother the earth, who sustains us and keeps us, and brings forth various fruits and flowers of many colours.

Praise and bless the Lord, and give thanks unto him, and serve him with great humility.

St Francis of Assisi

**He that is down need fear no fall,
he that is low no pride.**

John Bunyan

When [Jesus] was in the house He asked them, "What was it you disputed among yourselves on the road?" But they kept silent, for on the road they had disputed among themselves who would be the greatest. And He sat down, called the twelve, and said to them, "If anyone desires to be first, he shall be last of all and servant of all."

Mark 9:33–35

I used to think that God's gifts were on shelves one above the other and that the taller we grew in Christian character the more easily we could reach them. I now find that God's gifts are on shelves one beneath the other and that it is not a question of growing taller but of stooping lower.

Frederick Brotherton Meyer

All of you be submissive to one another, and be clothed with humility, for "God resists the proud, but gives grace to the humble." Therefore humble yourselves under the mighty hand of God, that He may exalt you in due time.

1 Peter 5:5–6

[God has] given to us exceedingly great and precious promises, that through these you may be partakers of the divine nature.

2 Peter 1:4

Well may grace be called the Divine nature, for as God brings light out of darkness, comfort out of sorrow, riches out of poverty, and glory out of shame, so does grace bring day out of night, and sweet out of bitter, and plenty out of poverty, and glory out of shame. It turns counters into gold, pebbles into pearls, sickness into health, weakness into strength, and wants into abundance; having nothing, and yet possessing all things.

Thomas Brooks

My God,
I pray that I may so know you and love you that I may rejoice in you.
And if I may not do so fully in this life, let me go steadily on to the day when I come to fullness of life.
Meanwhile let my mind meditate on your eternal goodness,
let my tongue speak of it,
let my heart live it,
let my mouth speak it,
let my soul hunger for it,
and my whole being desire it,
until I enter into your joy.

St Anselm of Canterbury

As the shadow of a great rock in a weary land.

Isaiah 32:2

In busy mart and crowded street,
No less than in the still retreat,
Thou, Lord, art near, our souls to bless,
With all a Father's tenderness.

Isaac Williams

Sooner or later, amidst the pleasures and the cares of ordinary life, the human spirit feels the need of a quiet, a comfort and a calm, beyond what anything in ordinary life can afford. In such seasons, there is one soft, restful shadow in the "weary land," and one only. It is in close personal union with him who has said, "Come unto me all you that labour and are heavy laden, and I will give you rest."[1]

His pardon for our sins, his sympathy in our troubles, his divine promises to believe in and dwell upon, himself to love and trust and have as our portion forever—in this is our rest.

Canon Wynne, adapted. [1]Matthew 11:28

Oh how divinely sweet it is to come into the secret of his presence, and abide in his pavilion!

David Brainerd

Great tempest, great calm; God proportions the comfort to the affliction.

Pasquier Quesnel

I waited patiently for the LORD;
And He inclined to me, and heard my cry.
He also brought me up out of a horrible pit,
Out of the miry clay,
And set my feet upon a rock,
And established my steps.

Psalm 40:1–2

A rock, though beaten on by winds and waves, is immoveable; so faith, grounded on the rock Christ, holds out in all temptations.

John Chrysostom

As the beautiful, dew-covered rose rises from amongst its thorns, so may my heart be so full of love for you, my God, that I may rise above the storms and evils that assail me, and stand fast in trust and freedom of spirit.

Hadewijch of Brabant

Hold fast the confidence and the rejoicing of the hope firm to the end.

Hebrews 3:6

Oh, give thanks to the LORD,
for He is good!
For His mercy endures forever.

1 Chronicles 16:34

By faith in Christ I walk with God,
With Heav'n, my journey's end, in view;
Supported by His staff and rod,
My road is safe and pleasant too.
I travel through a desert wide
Where many round me blindly stray;
But He vouchsafes to be my Guide,
And will not let me miss my way.

Though snares and dangers throng my path,
And earth and hell my course withstand;
I triumph over all by faith,
Guarded by His almighty hand.
With Him sweet converse I maintain,
Great as He is I dare be free;
I tell Him all my grief and pain,
And He reveals His love to me.

Some cordial from His Word He brings,
Whene'er my feeble spirit faints;
At once my soul revives and sings,
And yields no more to sad complaints.
Be this my choice, O Lord, to walk
With Thee, my Guide, my Guard, my Friend.

John Newton

The Word of God, Jesus Christ, out of his boundless love, became what we are, that he might make us what he is.

Irenaeus

Eternal depth of love divine,
In Jesus, God with us, displayed;
How bright Thy beaming glories shine!
How wide Thy healing streams are spread!

John Wesley

The love of God is one of the great realities of the universe, a pillar upon which the hope of the world rests. But it is a personal, intimate thing, too. God does not love populations, He loves people. He loves not masses, but men. He loves us all with a mighty love that has no beginning and can have no end.

Aiden Wilson Tozer

He loved us even to the death! May this love kindle ours; filling our souls with peace and joy; enabling us to resign grandeur, fame and pleasure; to count as nothing all that time shall destroy; to will the will of God, and to watch in unwearied and blissful expectation for the coming of the Lord.

François de la Mothe-Fénelon

Thank you for the beauty of this place

Yours, O LORD, is the greatness,
The power and the glory,
The victory and the majesty;
For all that is in heaven and in earth is Yours;
Yours is the kingdom, O LORD,
And You are exalted as head over all.

1 Chronicles 29:11

Lord and Father, we thank you for the beauty of this place that you created.

In all the uncertainties of our world, may the hills that stand steadfast and sure about us speak of the steadfastness of your love; may the sea around us with its eternal ebb and flow keep us aware of your ever-flowing grace; may the open sky above us remind us that your mercy is always offered to us.

Help us to remember that we are part of your creation and that you cherish us and hold us in the palm of your hand.

Prayer found at St. Tudno's Church, Wales; author unknown

In the morning the word of the LORD came to me.

Ezekiel 12:8

I met God in the morning,
When the day was at its best,
And His presence came like sunrise,
Like a glory in my breast.

All day long the presence lingered,
All day long He stayed with me,
And we sailed in perfect calmness
O'er a very troubled sea.

Ralph Spaulding Cushman

My soul hath desired thee all night, O eternal wisdom! And in the early morning I turn to thee from the depths of my heart. May the holy presence remove all dangers from my soul and body. May thy many graces fill my heart, and inflame it with thy divine love. O most sweet Jesus! Turn thy face towards me, for this morning with all the powers of my soul I fly to thee.

Henry Suso

You are my hope, O Lᴏʀᴅ God.

Psalm 71:5

The power of God is capable of finding hope where hope no longer exists, and a way where the way is impossible.

Gregory of Nyssa

Hope is a lover's staff; walk hence with that, and manage it against despairing thoughts.

William Shakespeare

I would say to my soul, O my soul, this is not the place of despair; this is not the time to despair in. As long as mine eyes can find a promise in the Bible, as long as there is a moment left me of breath or life in this world, so long will I wait or look for mercy, so long will I fight against unbelief and despair.

John Bunyan

Why are you cast down, O my soul?
And why are you disquieted within me?
Hope in God; For I shall yet praise Him,
The help of my countenance and my God.

Psalm 43:5

Jesus said to him, "I am the way, the truth, and the life. No one comes to the Father except through Me."

John 14:6

Christ is a free way; Christ is a near way; Christ is a firm way—there is no need of sinking; Christ is a pleasant way—"all thy ways are ways of pleasantness";[1] Christ is a safe way—there is a continual guard in that way; Christ is an easy way to hit—"wayfaring men, though fools, shall not err therein";[2] Christ is a spacious way—"thou hast set my feet in a large room."[3]

Tobias Crisp. [1] *Proverbs 3:17;* [2] *Isaiah 35:8;* [3] *Psalm 31:8*

The Word made flesh for us gives us the greatest hope that the murky night of darkness will not overwhelm us, but we shall see the daylight of eternity. Lord, let us receive your clear light; be for us such a mirror of light that we may be given grace to see you unendingly.

Hildegard of Bingen

Look up and lift up your heads, because your redemption draws near.

Luke 21:28

There was once a university professor who sprinkled his lectures with personal reflections that invariably began with, "As I was walking in my garden, it occurred to me that..." Over and over he passed on to his students thoughts that his garden had inspired.

One day he invited two of his most promising students to visit him at home, and over a cup of coffee the students asked to see his garden. To their amazement it was only a narrow strip, barely wider than the walkway, with the house on one side and a high wall on the other.

"Is this really the garden where you have all those inspiring thoughts, doctor?" one of the students asked.

"Yes," came the professor's reply.

"But it's so small!" protested the student.

"Ah, yes," said the professor, a twinkle in his eye as he gestured toward the sky, "but look how high it is!"

Retold

Learn from yesterday,
live for today, hope for tomorrow.

Albert Einstein

So, here hath been dawning
Another blue day.
Think, wilt thou let it
　Slip useless away?
Out of eternity
This new day is born;
Into eternity,
　At night, will return.
Behold it aforetime
No eye ever did:
So soon for it ever
　From all eyes is hid.
So, here hath been dawning
Another blue day.
Think, wilt thou let it
Slip useless away?

Thomas Carlyle

A daylily is a beautiful plant that has been cultivated for more than four thousand years. During its growing season, bright exotic flowers of serene white or gentle yellows, warm orange or vibrant reds blossom in the early morning only to wither away that evening. Each bloom has only been appointed one day in which to glow. That day is today.

A.M.

Do not be content with swimming on the surface of divine truth; make it your element; dive into it.

William Howells

The kingdom of heaven is like a merchant seeking beautiful pearls, who, when he had found one pearl of great price, went and sold all that he had and bought it.

Matthew 13:45–46

The glory of kings is to search out a matter.

Proverbs 25:2

Thy Word is like a deep, deep mine;
and jewels rich and rare
Are hidden in its mighty depths
        for every searcher there.

Edwin Hodder

O Lord, you have given us your word for a light to shine upon our path; inspire us to meditate on that word, and to follow its teaching, that we may find in it the light that shines more and more until the perfect day, through Jesus Christ our Lord.

Jerome

Teach me your way, O Lord;

I will walk in your truth; unite my heart to fear your name. Lead me, O Lord, in your righteousness; make your way straight before my face. Lead me in your truth and teach me, for you are the God of my salvation; on you I wait all the day. For you are my rock and my fortress; therefore, for your name's sake, lead me and guide me.

O Lord, you have searched me and known me. You know my sitting down and my rising up; you understand my thought afar off. You comprehend my path and my lying down, and are acquainted with all my ways. For there is not a word on my tongue, but behold, O Lord, you know it altogether.

Search me, O God, and know my heart; try me, and know my anxieties; and see if there is any wicked way in me, and lead me in the way everlasting. Teach me to do your will, for you are my God; your Spirit is good. Lead me in the land of uprightness.

Based on Psalm 86:11; 5:8; 25:5; 31:3; 139:1–4, 23–24; 143:10

The eyes of the LORD **are on the righteous,
And His ears are open to their cry.**

Psalm 34:15

Think of your worst moments, your sorrows, your losses, your sadness, and then remember that here you are, able to remember them. You got through the worst day of your life. You got through the trauma, you got through the trial, you endured the temptation, you survived the bad relationship, you're making your way out of the dark. Remember the bad things ... then look to see where you are. When we remember how difficult life used to be and how far we have come, we set up an explicit contrast in our mind, and this contrast is fertile ground for gratefulness.

Reverend Peter Gomes

If we will go with God upon the highway of love, we shall rest with him eternally and without end: and thus we shall eternally go forth towards God and enter into him and rest in him.

John of Ruysbroeck

I have set before you today life and good.

Deuteronomy 30:15

You had better live your best and act your best and think your best today; for today is the sure preparation for tomorrow and all the other tomorrows that follow.

Harriet Martineau

People sacrifice the present for the future. But life is available only in the present. That is why we should walk in such a way that every step can bring us to the here and the now.

Thich Nhat Hanh

Leave not the business of today to be done tomorrow; for who knows what may be your condition tomorrow? The rose-garden, which today is full of flowers, when tomorrow you would pluck a rose, may not afford you one.

Firdausī

To improve the golden moment of opportunity and catch the good that is within our reach, is the great art of life.

Samuel Johnson

Hold thy peace at the presence of the Lord GOD: for the day of the LORD is at hand.

Zephaniah 1:7 KJV

One who believes he is loved with an everlasting love, and knows that underneath are the everlasting arms, will find strength and peace.

Elisabeth Elliot

His forever, only His:
Who the Lord and me shall part?
Ah, with what a rest of bliss
Christ can fill the loving heart.
Things that once were wild alarms
Cannot now disturb my rest;
Closed in everlasting arms,
Pillowed on the loving breast.
Oh, to lie forever here,
Doubt and care and self resign,
While He whispers in my ear,
I am His, and He is mine.

George Wade Robinson

Let the weary, wandering soul bethink itself and retire to God. He will not mock thee with shadows as the world has done.

John Howe

Hope is like the sun, which, as we journey toward it, casts the shadow of our burden behind us.

Samuel Smiles

When Jesus had entered Capernaum, a centurion came to Him, pleading with Him, saying, "Lord, my servant is lying at home paralyzed, dreadfully tormented." And Jesus said to him, "I will come and heal him."

The centurion answered and said, "Lord, I am not worthy that You should come under my roof. But only speak a word, and my servant will be healed."

When Jesus heard it, He marveled, and said to those who followed, "Assuredly, I say to you, I have not found such great faith, not even in Israel!"

Then Jesus said to the centurion, "Go your way; and as you have believed, so let it be done for you." And his servant was healed that same hour.

Matthew 8:5–8,10,13

Though today may not fulfil
All your hopes, have patience still;
For perchance tomorrow's sun
Sees your happier days begun.

Author unknown

With you there is forgiveness.

Psalm 130:4

A young man, thin and bedraggled from his experiences of dire poverty, approaches with trepidation the home he had left long ago. His father, who has been going through years of anguish, sees him approach. The older man cannot wait a moment longer, but runs to greet him. His son had not yet spoken a word, but the father sees him "and has compassion", even crying tears of joy as he embraces his boy.

"When he was still a great way off, his father saw him and had compassion, and ran and fell on his neck and kissed him."[1]

What a picture of the unconditional love in God's heart. He doesn't wait for us to say exactly the right words; he doesn't look at our bedraggled state, nor how life has left us the worse for wear. He doesn't stand there chiding us for past mistakes and wrong decisions. No, from the moment we turn towards Him, He receives us with open arms.

A. M. [1]*Luke 15:20*

Restore us, O God; cause Your face to shine, and we shall be saved.

Psalm 80:3

Courage, brother! Do not stumble,
Though thy path is dark as night;

There's a star to guide the humble,
Trust in God and do the right.

Norman Macleod

Whatever you do, you need courage. Whatever course you decide upon, there is always someone to tell you that you are wrong. There are always difficulties arising that tempt you to believe your critics are right. To map out a course of action and follow it to an end requires some of the same courage that a soldier needs. Peace has its victories, but it takes brave men and women to win them.

Ralph Waldo Emerson

Courage may be loud and vigorous, but more often it is the silent conviction to take one step in front of another. Quiet determination to try again tomorrow is courage at its best.

A. M.

Jesus, Prince of Peace,
enter my soul with Your gift of peace.

But when you pray, go away by yourself, shut the door behind you, and pray to your Father in private. Then your Father, who sees everything, will reward you.

Matthew 6:6 NLT

Enter into the inner chamber of your mind. Shut out all things save God and whatever may aid you in seeking God; and having barred the door of your chamber, seek him.

St. Anselm of Canterbury

I don't say anything to God. I just sit there and look at him and let him look at me.

Author unknown

A poor life this if, full of care,
We have no time to stand and stare.

William Henry Davies

Contemplation is nothing else but a secret, peaceful, and loving infusion of God, which, if admitted, will set the soul on fire with the Spirit of love.

St John of the Cross

**You will keep him in perfect peace,
whose mind is stayed on You,
because he trusts in You.**

Isaiah 26:3

Always long and pray that the will of God may
be fully realised in your life. You will find that
the man who does this walks in the land of
peace and quietness.

Thomas à Kempis

Christ is the Way; he is also the Truth and the
Life. This power, this life, is within our reach
each moment of our life; as near, as free, as
abundant as the air we breathe. A breath of
prayer in the morning, and the morning life is
sure. A breath of prayer in the evening, and the
evening blessing comes.

Henry Drummond

Dear restless heart, be still,
    for peace is God's own smile,
His love can every wrong
    and sorrow reconcile;
Just love, and love, and love,
    and calmly wait awhile.

Edith Willis Linn

Therefore take heart, for I believe God that it
will be just as it was told me.

Acts 27:25

The humble He guides in justice,
and the humble He teaches His way.

Psalm 25:9

Lord, I ask you to give me a chance to be useful. Give me enough faith to believe You can do it. Enough love to put others before myself. Enough trust to share my limited material resources with those in need. Enough foresight to be of service. Enough strength to do what you inspire me to do today. Enough spiritual vitality to not neglect to pray for my family and colleagues. Enough patience to offer a listening ear. Enough kindness to pay attention to those around me.

Help me to live a worthwhile life, not necessarily through some great accomplishments (though I wouldn't mind if that was part of the plan), but most of all through a collection of small, loving and meaningful actions, day after day. Not for glory or reward, but because I want to follow in Your footsteps, The One who went everywhere doing good. Amen.

A vessel for honor, sanctified and useful for the Master, prepared for every good work.

2 Timothy 2:21

Let him who thirsts come.
Whoever desires,
let him take the water of life freely.

Revelation 22:17

From the watch of lonely mountain prayer,
   in gathering storm and blast—
From the path no mortal foot could tread,
   o'er waters wild and vast,
He came, the glorious Son of God,
   with healing, love and light,
To the land of far Gennesaret,
   that lay in shadowy night.

O Tender One, O Mighty One,
   who never sent away
The sinner or the sufferer,
   Thou art the same today!
The same in love, the same in power,
   and Thou art waiting still
To heal the multitudes that come,
   yea, 'whosoever will!'

Frances Ridley Havergal

When they had crossed over, they came to the land of Gennesaret. And when the men of that place recognized Him, they sent out into all that surrounding region, brought to Him all who were sick, and begged Him that they might only touch the hem of His garment. And as many as touched it were made perfectly well.

Matthew 14:34–36

The crowning of the year

You crown the year with Your goodness,
And Your paths drip with abundance.
They drop on the pastures
   of the wilderness,
And the little hills rejoice on every side.
The pastures are clothed with flocks;
The valleys also are covered with grain;
They shout for joy, they also sing.

Psalm 65:11–13

Think of the number of trees and blades of grass and flowers, the extravagant wealth of beauty no one ever sees! Think of the sunrises and sunsets we never look at! God is lavish in every degree.

Oswald Chambers

We thank thee then, O Father,
For all things bright and good;
The seed-time and the harvest,
Our life, our health, our food.

No gifts have we to offer
For all thy love imparts,
But that which thou desirest,
Our humble, thankful hearts.

Matthias Claudius

O LORD **God,**
please give me success this day.

Genesis 24:12

One today is worth two tomorrows.

Francis Quarles

Know the true value of time; snatch, seize and enjoy every moment of it.—No idleness, no delay, no procrastination; never put off till tomorrow what you can do today.

Philip D. S. Chesterfield

Men spend their lives in anticipations, in determining to be vastly happy at some period when they have time. But the present time has one advantage over every other—it is our own. Past opportunities are gone, future are not yet come. We may lay in a stock of pleasures, as we would lay in a stock of wine; but if we defer the tasting of them too long, we shall find that both are soured by age.

Caleb C. Colton

Happy the man, and happy he alone,
He who can call today his own;
He who, secure within, can say,
To-morrow, do thy worst, for I have liv'd today.

John Dryden

The eternal God is your refuge,
And underneath are the everlasting arms.

Deuteronomy 33:27

Behold the love of God. In those years that have passed away, it never failed. When we fell, it raised us; when we wandered, it recalled us; when we fainted, it revived us; when we sinned, it pardoned us; when we wept, it comforted us. In those moments of agony and doubt and almost despair, which some can recall, it was all-sufficient.

Rev Canon Money, adapted

O God, whose smile is in the sky,
Whose path is in the sea,
Once more from earth's tumultuous strife
We gladly turn to thee.

We come as those with toil far spent
Who crave thy rest and peace,
And from the care and fret of life
Would find in thee release.

John H. Holmes

What I have, I give you.

One day Peter and John were going up to the temple at the time of prayer – at three in the afternoon. Now a man who was lame from birth was being carried to the temple gate called Beautiful, where he was put every day to beg from those going into the temple courts. When he saw Peter and John about to enter, he asked them for money. Peter looked straight at him, as did John. Then Peter said, 'Look at us!' So the man gave them his attention, expecting to get something from them.

Then Peter said, 'Silver or gold I do not have, but what I do have I give you. In the name of Jesus Christ of Nazareth, walk.'

Taking him by the right hand, he helped him up, and instantly the man's feet and ankles became strong. He jumped to his feet and began to walk. Then he went with them into the temple courts, walking and jumping, and praising God.

Acts 3:3–8

We all have something to give. It might not be wealth or miracles, but we can take another by the hand of love.

A. M.

I will give thanks to You, O LORD **...**
And sing praises to Your name.

2 Samuel 22:50

GATHERED to Thy name, Lord Jesus,
Losing sight of all but Thee,
Oh, what joy Thy presence gives us,
Calling up our hearts to Thee!
Oh, the joy, the wondrous singing
When we see Thee as Thou art,
Thy blest name, Lord Jesus, bringing
Sweetest music to God's heart!
Notes of gladness, songs unceasing,
Hymns of everlasting praise,
Psalms of glory, joy increasing,
Through God's endless day of days!

C. A. Wellesley

Make a joyful shout to the L ORD,
all you lands!
Serve the LORD with gladness;
Come before His presence with singing.
Enter into His gates with thanksgiving,
And into His courts with praise.
Be thankful to Him, and bless His name.

Psalm 100:1–2,4

**Trust the past to God's mercy,
the present to God's love,
and the future to God's providence.**

St Augustine of Hippo

It happened, as [Jesus] was coming near Jericho, that a certain blind man sat by the road begging, and he cried out, saying, "Jesus, Son of David, have mercy on me!"

And when [Jesus] had come near, He asked him, saying, "What do you want Me to do for you?" He said, "Lord, that I may receive my sight."

Then Jesus said to him, "Receive your sight; your faith has made you well."

And immediately he received his sight, and followed Him, glorifying God.

Luke 18:35–42

How often we look upon God as our last and feeblest resource! We go to him because we have nowhere else to go. And then we learn that the storms of life have driven us, not upon the rocks, but into the desired haven.

George MacDonald

**Prayer is the key to open the day,
and the bolt to shut in the night.**

Jeremy Taylor

Whatever it is that presses you, go tell your Father; put the matter into His hand, and so you will be freed from that perplexing care that the world is full of. When you are either to do or suffer anything, when you are about any purpose or business, go tell God of it, and acquaint Him with it; yes, burden Him with it, and you have done all you need for the matter of caring. ... Roll your cares, and yourself with them, as one burden, all on your God.

Robert Leighton, adapted

Dear Jesus, I want each day that comes
To share some part with you,
Where I can sit, receive your peace,
And hear you speak to me.

A place where I can turn aside
And leave the cares of life,
Where I can get the strength I need
To banish storm and strife.

A quiet, serene and trusting place
Where you alone can give
The very blessing that I need—
Here would I rest and live.

Author unknown

It is the Spirit who gives life; the flesh profits nothing. The words that I speak to you are spirit, and they are life.

John 6:63

A man may read the figures on the sundial, but he cannot tell how the day goes unless the sun is shining on it; so we may read the Bible over, but we cannot learn its purpose till the spirit of God shines upon it and into our hearts.

Thomas Watson

The Bible is the light of my understanding, the joy of my heart, the fullness of my hope, the clarifier of my affections, the mirror of my thoughts, the consoler of my sorrows, the guide of my soul through this gloomy labyrinth of time, the telescope sent from heaven to reveal to the eye of man the amazing glories of the far distant world.

Sir William Jones

Lead me in Your truth and teach me,
For You are the God of my salvation;
On You I wait all the day.

Psalm 25:5

There was a calm

Now it happened, on a certain day, that He got into a boat with His disciples. And He said to them, "Let us cross over to the other side of the lake." And they launched out.

But as they sailed He fell asleep. And a windstorm came down on the lake, and they were filling with water, and were in jeopardy.

And they came to Him and awoke Him, saying, "Master, Master, we are perishing!" Then He arose and rebuked the wind and the raging of the water. And they ceased, and there was a calm.

Luke 8:22–24

Nothing does so much establish the mind amidst the rollings and turbulency of present things, as both a look above them, and a look beyond them; above them to the good and steady Hand by which they are ruled, and beyond them to the sweet and beautiful end to which, by that Hand, they shall be brought.

Attributed to Jeremy Taylor

The manifestations of the power of God, like His mercies, are "new every morning" and fresh every moment.

Daniel Webster

Through the Lord's mercies
we are not consumed,
Because His compassions fail not.
They are new every morning;
Great is Your faithfulness.

Lamentations 3:22–23

There's a wideness in God's mercy,
Like the wideness of the sea;
There's a kindness in His justice,
Which is more than liberty.
For the love of God is broader
Than the measure of our mind;
And the heart of the Eternal
Is most wonderfully kind.

Frederick William Faber

Many, O Lord my God,
are Your wonderful works
Which You have done;
And Your thoughts toward us
Cannot be recounted to You in order;
If I would declare and speak of them,
They are more than can be numbered.

Psalm 40:5

The just shall live by his faith.

Habakkuk 2:4

Faith is to believe what you do not yet see: the reward for this faith is to see what you believe.

Augustine of Hippo

Faith is the foot of the soul by which it can march along the road of the commandments. Love can make the feet move more swiftly, but faith is the foot that carries the soul. With faith I can do all things; without faith I shall neither have the inclination nor the power to do anything in the service of God. If you would find the men who serve God the best, you must look for the men of the most faith. Little faith will save a man, but little faith cannot do great things for God.

Charles Haddon Spurgeon

Faith is the eye that sees him, the hand that clings to him, the receiving power that appropriates him.

John E. Woodbridge

Ageless

Then said I: "Ah, Lord GOD! Behold, I cannot speak, for I am a youth."

But the LORD said to me: "Do not say, 'I am a youth,' For you shall go to all to whom I send you, And whatever I command you, you shall speak. Do not be afraid of their faces. For I am with you to deliver you," says the LORD.

Jeremiah 1:6–8

Finding meaning and fullness of life has nothing to do with age. God is not limited by our age or experience, not limited by many or by few.[1] Gideon won a major battle with only 300 men and some motley weapons: torches, trumpets and empty clay jars.[2] Jesus fed the multitude with a boy's lunch.[3] Whoever you are and at whatever stage of life, never allow yourself to be intimidated; go forward with God's support and there will be no stopping you.

A.M. [1] 1 Samuel 14:6; [2] Judges 6 and 7; [3] John 6:5–13

The greater and more persistent your confidence in God, the more abundantly you will receive all that you ask.

Albert the Great

Go therefore.

Matthew 28:19

Green light – it's time to go. There is a lot of "going" in the Gospel narrative. Labourers are sent into the vineyard,[1] freshly healed lepers are sent to the temple,[2] the disciples are sent out preaching and teaching.[3] Jesus Himself stayed on the move: "Jesus went about all the cities and villages, teaching in their synagogues, preaching the gospel of the kingdom, and healing every sickness and every disease among the people."[4] It wasn't activity simply for the sake of staying busy, but purposeful, meaningful action.

God calls us to activity. Our response to the needs around us should be more than sympathy, but action.[5]

A.M. [1] Matthew 20:6–7, [2] Luke 17:12–14, [3] Matthew 10:7, [4] Matthew 9:35, [5] James 2:15–16

We cannot live only for ourselves. A thousand fibers connect us with our fellow-men; and along those fibers, as sympathetic threads, our actions run as causes, and they come back to us as effects.

Herman Melville

My prayer

Give me, good Lord, a humble, lowly, quiet, peaceable, patient, charitable, kind, tender and pitiful mind, in all my works and all my words and all my thoughts, to have a taste of your holy, blessed Spirit.

Give me, good Lord, a full faith, a firm hope and a fervent charity, a love of you incomparably above the love of myself.

Give me, good Lord, a longing to be with you, not to void the calamities of this world, nor so much to attain the joys of heaven, as simply for love of you.

And give me, good Lord, your love and favour, which my love of you, however great it might be, could not deserve were it not for your great goodness.

These things, good Lord, that I pray for, give me your grace to labour for.

Thomas More

**Great is the LORD,
and greatly to be praised;
and His greatness is unsearchable.**

Psalm 145:3

I am not so much of a farmer as some people claim, but I have observed the watermelon seed. It has the power of drawing from the ground and through itself 200,000 times its weight. When you can tell me how it takes this material and out of it colors an outside surface beyond the imitation of art, and then forms inside of it a white rind and within again a red heart, thickly inlaid with black seeds, each one of which in turn is capable of drawing through itself 200,000 times its weight. When you can explain to me the mystery of a watermelon, you can ask me to explain the mystery of God.

William Jennings Bryan

We don't know the millionth part of one percent about anything. We don't know what water is. We don't know what light is. We don't know what gravitation is. We don't know what heat is. But we do not let our ignorance about these things deprive us of their use.

Thomas Alva Edison

These things I command you,
that you love one another.

John 15:17

The more you love, the more love you are given to love with.

Lucian Price

Kind words are the flowers in life's garden, bringing scent and colour to the landscape.

A. M.

Love is the shortest and swiftest way to God.

Johannes Tauler

O God of love, we ask you to give us love;
Love in our thinking, love in our speaking,
Love in our doing,
And love in the hidden places of our souls;
Love of those with whom
we find it hard to bear,
And love of those
who find it hard to bear with us;
Love of those with whom we work,
And love of those
with whom we take our ease;
That so at length
we may be worthy to dwell with you,
Who are eternal love.

William Temple

In the chamber

[At the house] he saw a tumult and those who wept and wailed loudly. He said to them, "Why make this commotion and weep? The child is not dead, but sleeping." When He had put them all outside, He took the father and the mother of the child, and those who were with Him, and entered where the child was lying. Then He took the child by the hand, and said to her, "Little girl, I say to you, arise." Immediately the girl arose and walked.

Mark 5:38–42, abridged

If we let God's thoughts, as they are revealed in the Word, come in and fill the chamber of our minds, our views and feelings regarding both God and ourselves will be so different! If we let God's thoughts in, it will be like Jesus coming into the midst of the mourners and saying, "Why are you making such a commotion, and weeping? The damsel is not dead, but sleeping."[1]

As the minstrels and other mourners were put out of the house by Jesus, so must our thoughts be put out of our hearts by God's thoughts. Then, all being still, the sweet voice of the Redeemer will be heard, "Maid, arise!"

William Hepburn Hewitson, adapted. [1]*Mark 5:39*

O Lord GOD, You are God, and Your words are true.

2 Samuel 7:28

There is abundant evidence that the Bible, though written by men, is not the product of the human mind. By countless multitudes it has always been revered as a communication to us from the Creator of the universe.

Sir Ambrose Fleming

For me, the Bible is the Book. I cannot see how anybody can live without it.

Gabriela Mistral

The Bible is a rock of diamonds, a chain of pearls, the sword of the Spirit; a chart by which the Christian sails to eternity; the map by which he daily walks; the sundial by which he sets his life; the balance in which he weighs his actions.

Thomas Watson

Every word of God is pure;
He is a shield to those who put their trust in Him.

Proverbs 30:5

Whatever you ask the Father in My name He may give you.

John 15:16

Imagine what would happen if you went to a friend in the middle of the night and said, 'Friend, lend me three loaves of bread. An old friend traveling through just showed up, and I don't have a thing on hand.'

The friend answers from his bed, 'Don't bother me. The door's locked; my children are all down for the night; I can't get up to give you anything.' But let me tell you, even if he won't get up because he's a friend, if you stand your ground, knocking and waking all the neighbors, he'll finally get up and get you whatever you need.

Here's what I'm saying:

Ask and you'll get;
Seek and you'll find;
Knock and the door will open.

Don't bargain with God. Be direct. Ask for what you need.

Luke 11:5–10 MSG

It is because God has promised certain things that we can ask for them with the full assurance of faith.

Aiden Wilson Pink

Let us not grow weary while doing good, for in due season we shall reap if we do not lose heart.

Galatians 6:9

Never look down to test the ground before taking your next step; only he who keeps his eye fixed on the far horizon will find the right road.

Dag Hammarskjold

A single stroke of an axe won't bring down an oak, but many will.

Spanish proverb

All that I have accomplished, or expect or hope to accomplish, has been and will be by that plodding, patient, persevering process of accumulation that builds the ant-heap, particle by particle, thought by thought, fact by fact.

Elihu Burritt

Here is the great secret of success: Work with all your might, but never trust in your work. Pray with all your might for the blessing in God, but work at the same time with all diligence, with all patience, with all perseverance. Pray and work. Work and pray.

George Müller

Out in the fields with God

The flowers appear on the earth;
The time of singing has come,
And the voice of the turtledove
Is heard in our land.
The fig tree puts forth her green figs,
And the vines with the tender grapes
Give a good smell.

Song of Solomon 2:12–13

The little cares that fretted me,
I lost them yesterday,
Among the fields above the sea,
Among the winds at play;
Among the lowing of the herds,
The rustling of the trees;
Among the singing of the birds,
The humming of the bees.

The foolish fears of what might happen,
I cast them all away
Among the clover-scented grass,
Among the new-mown hay;
Among the husking of the corn,
Where drowsy poppies nod,
Where ill thoughts die and good are born—
Out in the fields with God!

Elizabeth Barrett Browning

He who has seen Me has seen the Father.

John 14:9

Kedleston Hall in the rolling green hills of England was the work of craftsmen in centuries past; visitors today admire the panelled walls and exquisite paintings. The elaborate patterns on the high-domed plaster ceiling in the saloon can best be examined by gazing into mirrors placed strategically on the floor. The mirrors reflect and bring into plain view the intricate designs that would otherwise be too distant to appreciate.

God is too great for our sight; we cannot focus upon him. He is too high. Jesus is like the mirror; in him we see God's reflection.

A. M.

Jesus brings God into our world and within our reach. He enables us to know what God is like. God is in heaven, but we see his reflection in Jesus.

John MacBeath

**Bless the Lord, O my soul,
and forget not all His benefits.**

Psalm 103:2

When you have eaten and are satisfied, praise the Lord your God for the good land he has given you.

Deuteronomy 8:10

We pray for the big things and forget to give thanks for the ordinary, small (and yet really not small) gifts.

Dietrich Bonhoeffer

Begin by thanking Him for some little thing, and then go on, day by day, adding to your subjects of praise; thus you will find their numbers grow wonderfully; and, in the same proportion, will your subjects of murmuring and complaining diminish, until you see in everything some cause for thanksgiving.

Priscilla Maurice

Thankfulness is the secret of joy.

Author unknown

Oh, that men would give thanks to the Lord for His goodness, and for His wonderful works to the children of men!

Psalm 107:8

I reckon that the sufferings of this present time are not worthy to be compared with the glory which shall be revealed in us.

Romans 8:18 (AV)

Christian, why weepest thou? Look up! Heaven is smiling above you! Look around! Heaven is opening before you! Let your tears, if they must fall, be as the drops of rain which fall in the sunshine and reflect the colours of the rainbow. The last year of earth will soon be wiped away, amid the first smile of heaven; and that smile will be eternal.

John Angell James

O Lord,
The help of the helpless,
The hope of the hopeless,
The saviour of the storm-tossed,
The harbour of voyagers,
The physician of the sick;
We pray to you.

O Lord,
You know each of us and our petitions;
You know each house and its needs;
Receive us all into your kingdom;
Make us children of light,
And bestow your peace and love upon us.

Basil of Caesarea

How far that little candle throws his beams! So shines a good deed in a naughty world.

William Shakespeare

Neither do men light a candle, and put it under a bushel, but on a candlestick; and it gives light unto all that are in the house. Let your light so shine before men, that they may see your good works, and glorify your Father which is in heaven.

Matthew 5:15–16

Happiness is a sunbeam which may pass through a thousand [hearts] without losing a particle of its original ray; nay, when it strikes on a kindred heart, like the converged light on a mirror, it reflects itself with redoubled brightness.—It is not perfected till it is shared.

Jane Porter

For You will light my lamp;
The LORD my God will enlighten my darkness.

Psalm 18:28

Pay attention, come close now, listen carefully to my life-giving, life-nourishing words.

Isaiah 55:3 MSG

[Martha] had a sister called Mary, who also sat at Jesus' feet and heard His word. But Martha was distracted with much serving, and she approached Him and said, "Lord, do You not care that my sister has left me to serve alone? Therefore tell her to help me."

And Jesus answered and said to her, "Martha, Martha, you are worried and troubled about many things. But one thing is needed, and Mary has chosen that good part, which will not be taken away from her."

Luke 10:39–42

Martha was someone who missed out on the peace and inspiration that Jesus gives on at least one occasion. She was presumably a successful housekeeper, but in the hurry and flurry of her busy activities, she didn't make time for Him. One thing was needed: to listen.

A. M.

My beloved spoke and said to me, `Arise, my darling, my beautiful one, come with me.'

Song of Solomon 2:10

While I live I will praise the LORD;
I will sing praises to my God while I have
my being.

Psalm 146:2

I know nothing more constant to expel the sadness of the world than to sound out the praises of God as with a trumpet; and when the heart is cast down, this will make it rebound from earth to heaven.

Jeremy Taylor

When thankfulness o'erflows the swelling heart, and breathes in free and uncorrupted praise for benefits received, propitious heaven takes such acknowledgement as fragrant incense, and doubles all its blessings.

George Lillo

Joy is the echo of God's life within us.

Joseph Marmion

I'll lift my hands, I'll raise my voice,
 While I have breath to pray or praise;
This work shall make my heart rejoice
 And spend the remnant of my days.

Isaac Watts

All Your billows and Your waves passed over me.

Jonah 2:3

The Lord lead thee, day by day, in the right way, and keep thy mind stayed upon Him, in whatever befalls thee; that the belief of His love and hope in His mercy, when thou art at the lowest ebb, may keep up thy head above the billows.

Isaac Penington

The Lord himself goes before you and will be with you; he will never leave you nor forsake you. Do not be afraid; do not be discouraged.

Deuteronomy 31:8

Say to those who are fearful-hearted, "Be strong, do not fear! Behold, your God ... will come and save you."

Isaiah 35:4

What's more, I am with you, and I will protect you wherever you go. ... I will not leave you until I have finished giving you everything I have promised you.

Genesis 28:15 NLT

**Out of Zion, the perfection of beauty,
God will shine forth.**

Psalm 50:2

[But God has] raised us up together, and made us sit together in the heavenly places in Christ Jesus, that in the ages to come He might show the exceeding riches of His grace in His kindness toward us in Christ Jesus.

Ephesians 2:6–7

O Jesus, Friend unfailing,
How dear you are to me!
Are cares or fears assailing?
I find my strength in thee!

For every tribulation,
For every sore distress,
In Christ I've full salvation,
Sure help and quiet rest.

No fear of foes prevailing,
I triumph, Lord, in thee!
O Jesus, Friend unfailing,
How dear you are to me!

Samuel C.G. Kaester, adapted

You will find him an unfading flower in a fading world.

James Harrington Evans

In returning and rest you shall be saved.

Isaiah 30:15

Enter this wild wood and view the haunts of nature. The calm shade shall bring a kindred calm, and the sweet breeze that makes the green leaves dance shall waft a balm to thy sick heart.

William Cullen Bryant

The best remedy for those who are afraid, lonely or unhappy is to go outside, somewhere where they can be quiet, alone with the heavens, nature and God. Because only then does one feel that all is as it should be and that God wishes to see people happy, amidst the simple beauty of nature.

Anne Frank

Lonely woods with paths dim and silent,
A haunt of peace for weary hearted.
There's healing in your shade,
And in your stillness balm.
Here seek repose
From the world's strife and glamour,
Find a haven calm and secure
And go forward strengthened and renewed.

Jean-Baptiste de Lully

Life is a flower of which love is the honey.

Victor Hugo

Two are better than one,
Because they have a good reward
   for their labor.
For if they fall,
   one will lift up his companion.
But woe to him who is alone when he falls,
   For he has no one to help him up.

Again, if two lie down together,
   they will keep warm;
But how can one be warm alone?
Though one may be overpowered
   by another,
   two can withstand him.
And a threefold cord is not quickly broken.

Ecclesiastes 4:9–12

A solitary blessing few can find;
Our joys with those we love are intertwined;
And he, whose wakeful tenderness removes
Th' obstructing thorn which wounds the friend
he loves,
Smooths not another's rugged path alone,
But scatters roses to adorn his own.

Hannah More

For this is the message that you heard from the
beginning, that we should love one another.

1 John 3:11

By perseverance the snail reached the ark.

Charles Haddon Spurgeon

Our heart has not turned back,
Nor have our steps departed from Your way.

Psalm 44:18

Everyone who achieves success in a great venture, solves each problem as they came to it. They helped themselves. And they were helped through powers known and unknown to them at the time they set out on their voyage. They keep going regardless of the obstacles they met.

W. Clement Stone

I try to avoid looking forward or backward, and try to keep looking upward.

Charlotte Brontë

Build to-day, then, strong and sure,
With a firm and ample base;
And ascending and secure
Shall to-morrow find its place.

Henry Wadsworth Longfellow

Walk worthy of the Lord, fully pleasing Him, being fruitful in every good work and increasing in the knowledge of God.

Colossians 1:10

In all hard work there is profit.

Proverbs 14:23 WEB

An elderly carpenter was ready to retire. When he told his boss his plans, the contractor was sorry to see such a good worker go, and he asked the carpenter to build just one more house as a personal favour.

The carpenter agreed, but his heart was not in his work. He resorted to shoddy workmanship and used inferior materials.

When he had finished, the employer came to inspect the house. He handed the front-door key to the carpenter. "This is your house," he said. "It is my gift to you."

The carpenter was shocked! What a shame! If he had only known he was building his own house, he would have done it all so differently.

So it is with us. We build our lives, a day at a time, often putting less than our best into the building. Then with a shock we realise we have to live in the house we have built. If we could do it over, we'd do it much differently. But we cannot go back.

You are the carpenter of your life. Each day you hammer a nail, place a board, or erect a wall. Your attitudes and the choices you make today build your "house" for tomorrow. Build wisely!

Author unknown

Remade

I went down to the potter's house, and there he was, making something at the wheel. And the vessel that he made of clay was marred in the hand of the potter; so he made it again into another vessel, as it seemed good to the potter to make.

Jeremiah 18:3–4

This world is God's workshop for making men in.

Henry Ward Beecher

You are surprised at your imperfections—why? Surely, you might rather be astonished that you do not fall into more frequent and more grievous faults, and thank God for His upholding grace.

Jean Nicolas Grou

Don't waste energy trying to cover up failure. Learn from your failures and go on to the next challenge. It's okay to fail. If you're not failing, you're not growing.

H. Stanley Judd

It is the nature of God to make something out of nothing; therefore, when anyone is nothing, God may yet make something of him.

Martin Luther

At the start of the day

Struggling to start your day? Perhaps it's not coffee you need but something else: "The very moment you wake up each morning ... all your wishes and hopes for the day rush at you like wild animals. And the first job each morning consists simply in shoving them all back; in listening to that other voice, taking that other point of view, letting that other larger, stronger, quieter life come flowing in."—So advises C. S. Lewis.

A. M.

I will begin here also with the beginning of time, the morning; so soon as you wake, retire your mind into a pure silence from all thoughts and ideas of worldly things, and in that frame wait upon God to feel his good presence, to lift up your hearts to him, and commit your whole self into his blessed care and protection.

William Penn

O secret Christ,
Lord of the rose of dawn,
    hide me within thy silent peace,
that, throughout the turmoil of the day,
I may abide within
    the quiet of the daybreak.

Used in the chapel at Launde Abbey, author unknown.

Jesus answered and said to them, "Have faith in God."

Mark 11:22

Faith is the hand by which we may hold on to Jesus.

Jean Mestrezat

Faith makes God and man good friends; faith brings God and man together.

Patrick Hamilton

Faith is the door whereby we enter into the house of God.

Desiderius Erasmus

Faith in Jesus Christ is the soul's flight into the city of refuge.

Hugh Binning

Behold, Lord, an empty vessel that needs to be filled. My Lord, fill it. I am weak in the faith; strengthen me. I am cold in love; warm me and make me fervent that my love may go out to my neighbour. I do not have a strong and firm faith; at times I doubt and am unable to trust you altogether. O Lord, help me and strengthen my faith and trust in you.

Martin Luther

**The heavens declare the glory of God,
And the sky proclaims the work of His
hands.**

Psalm 19:1 CSB

A star-filled sky is a picture of hope; twinkles of
light in the dark of distant space remind us that
we are never alone.

A. M.

God of the earth, the sky, the sea!
Maker of all above, below!
Creation lives and moves in Thee,
Thy present life in all doth flow.

Samuel Longfellow

My dearest Lord,
be now a bright flame to enlighten me,
a guiding star to lead me,
a smooth path beneath my feet,
and a kindly shepherd along my way,
today and for evermore.

Columba

The way

Now I will teach thee the way of peace and inward liberty. Be desirous to do the will of another rather than thine own. Choose always to have less rather than more. Seek always the lowest place and to be inferior to everyone. Wish always, and pray, that the will of God may be wholly fulfilled in thee.

Thomas à Kempis

Imitate God, therefore, in everything you do, because you are his dear children. Live a life filled with love, following the example of Christ. He loved us and offered himself as a sacrifice for us, a pleasing aroma to God.

Be careful how you live. Don't live like fools, but like those who are wise. Make the most of every opportunity in these evil days. Don't act thoughtlessly, but understand what the Lord wants you to do.

Ephesians 5:1–3, 16–18 NLT

May God himself, the God who makes everything holy and whole, make you holy and whole, put you together—spirit, soul, and body—and keep you fit for the coming of our Master, Jesus Christ. The One who called you is completely dependable. If he said it, he'll do it!

1 Thessalonians 5:23–24 MSG

When they had read it, they rejoiced over its encouragement.

Acts 15:31

Literacy gives the reader access to the mind and thoughts of people the world over, from the past to the present. It opens a universe of knowledge. What's more, literacy gives us access to God's thoughts, as revealed through the Bible and the inspired writers of all time.

The Bible abounds with literacy events, ranging from public readings, such as Moses reading the book of the Covenant aloud to the people[1] and Jesus reading from the book of Isaiah in the synagogue,[2] to admonitions to quiet, meditative reading.[3] According to Revelation 20:12, there are apparently even books in heaven itself: "Books were opened." Literacy lasts forever.

A. M. [1]Exodus 24:7; [2]Luke 4:17; [3]Deuteronomy 17:19

Ezra opened the book in the sight of all the people. ... So [*the leaders*] read distinctly from the book, in the Law of God; and they gave the sense, and helped them to understand the reading.

Nehemiah 8:5,8

Behold! The Lamb of God who takes away the sin of the world!

John 1:29

Rest of the weary,
Joy of the sad,
Hope of the dreary,
Light of the glad;
Home of the stranger,
Strength to the end,
Refuge from danger,
Saviour and Friend!

Author unknown

Christ willed to become what man is, in order that man might become what Christ is.

Cyprian of Carthage

To me, Jesus is the Life I want to live, the Light I want to reflect, the Way to the Father, the Love I want to express, the Joy I want to share, the Peace I want to sow around me. Jesus is everything to me.

Mother Teresa

Fashion in me, Lord, eyes within my eyes,
so that, with new eyes,
I may contemplate your divine sacrifice.
Create in me a pure heart,
so that, through the power of your Spirit,
I may inhale your salvation.

Joseph the Visionary

For no sooner has the sun risen with a burning heat than it withers the grass; its flower falls, and its beautiful appearance perishes.

James 1:11

It is fair, that lily dressed by God, but it fades. He only intended its beauty to be for a day; all our earthly joy he intends for a similar short duration. Its earthly part, like the petals of the flower, must droop and disappear.

This is not our home, nor our rest. But underneath, growing and strengthening in the Christian's daily life, there is a joy that will never fade and a beauty that will never be dimmed. His life is "hid with Christ in God."[1]

The joy he has in his Saviour's love, the joy he shares—that joy no one can take away. It is not an earthly but a celestial flower, and it will bloom hereafter in the paradise of God with a splendour and fragrance that it has not entered into the heart of man to conceive.

Canon Wynne, adapted. [1]*Colossians 3:3*

Let all those rejoice who put their trust in You;
Let them ever shout for joy, because You defend them;
Let those also who love Your name
Be joyful in You.

Psalm 5:11

Revive me according to Your lovingkindness.

Psalm 119:88

Though waves and storms go o'er my head,
Though strength and health
    and friends be gone.
Though joys be withered all, and dead,
Though every comfort be withdrawn,
On this my steadfast soul relies,--
Father! Thy mercy never dies.

Johann A. Röthe

God of our life, there are days when the burdens we carry chafe our shoulders and weigh us down; when the road seems dreary and endless, the skies gray and threatening; when our lives have no music in them, and our hearts are lonely, and our souls have lost their courage.

Flood the path with light; run our eyes to where the skies are full of promise; tune our hearts to brave music; give us the sense of comradeship with heroes and saints of every age; and so revive our spirits that we may be able to encourage the souls of all who journey with us on the road of life, to your honour and glory.

Attributed to Augustine

Let us run with patience the race that is set before us.

Hebrews 12:1 KJV

Have courage for the great sorrows of life, and patience for the small ones. And when you have laboriously accomplished your daily task, go to sleep in peace. God is awake.

Victor Hugo

He said not, 'Thou shalt not be tempested, thou shalt not be travailed, thou shalt not be afflicted,' but he said, 'Thou shalt not be overcome.'

Julian of Norwich

Let us belong to God even in the thick of the disturbance up round about us by the diversity of human affairs. True virtue is not always nourished in external calm any more than good fish are always found in stagnant waters.

Francis de Sales

Dost thou not know that thy God loves thee in the midst of all this? Mountains, when in darkness hidden, are as real as in day, and God's love is as true to thee now as it was in thy brightest moments.

Charles Haddon Spurgeon

I will never leave you nor forsake you.

Hebrews 13:5

Abide in Me, and I in you.

John 15:4

In its archaic meaning, to abide is to reside or to live. Edward M. Blaiklock described abiding in Christ with these words: "Experience God's presence by an unbroken attitude of mind; visualise God within; remember that he is the hearer of all speech, the monitor of all thoughts, the judge of all actions. Then you will precisely 'abide in Christ.'"

It takes faith as well as practical effort to live in Christ, but the reward is peace.

A. M.

O my God, Trinity whom I adore, let me entirely forget myself that I may abide in you, still and peaceful as if my soul were already in eternity; let nothing disturb my peace nor separate me from you, O my unchanging God, but that each moment may take me further into the depths of your mystery.

Elizabeth of the Trinity

I am resting

Jesus, I am resting, resting,
In the joy of what thou art;
I am finding out the greatness
Of thy loving heart.

Jean Sophia Pigott

One thing I have desired of you, that will I seek: that I may dwell in your house all the days of my life, to behold your beauty, and to inquire in your temple. For in the time of trouble you shall hide me in your pavilion; in the secret place of your tabernacle you shall hide me; you will set me high upon a rock. And now my head shall be lifted up; therefore I will offer sacrifices of joy in your presence; I will sing, yes, I will sing praises to you.

Adapted from Psalm 27:4–6

Lord, be within me
—To strengthen me; without me
—To preserve me; over me
—To shelter me; beneath me
—To support me; before me
—To direct me; behind me
—To bring me back; around me
—To fortify me.

Lancelot Andrews

The salvation of the righteous is from the LORD; He is their strength in the time of trouble.

Psalm 37:39

There is a place of quiet rest,
Near to the heart of God.
A place where sin cannot molest,
Near to the heart of God.

O Jesus, blest Redeemer,
Sent from the heart of God,
Hold us who wait before Thee
Near to the heart of God.

There is a place of comfort sweet,
Near to the heart of God.
A place where we our Saviour meet,
Near to the heart of God.

There is a place of full release,
Near to the heart of God.
A place where all is joy and peace,
Near to the heart of God.

Cleland Boyd McAfee

I will both lie down in peace, and sleep;
For You alone, O LORD, make me dwell in safety.

Psalm 4:8

His friends

A certain centurion's servant, who was dear to him, was sick and ready to die. The centurion sent friends to [*Jesus*], saying to Him,

"Lord, do not trouble Yourself, for I am not worthy that You should enter under my roof. But say the word, and my servant will be healed."

When Jesus heard these things, He marveled at him. And those who were sent, returning to the house, found the servant well who had been sick.

Luke 7:2–10

I am not worthy, Master and Lord, that you should come beneath the roof of my soul; yet since in your love towards all, you wish to dwell in me, in boldness I come. You command; open the gates, which you alone have made. And you will come in, and enlighten my darkened reasoning. I believe that you will do this; for you did not send away the harlot who came to you with tears, nor cast out the repenting tax-collector, nor reject the thief who acknowledged your kingdom. But you counted all of these as members of your band of friends. You are blessed for evermore.

John Chrysostom

Though I walk in the midst of trouble, You will revive me.

Psalm 138:7

The bright rays of a golden sun illuminate the journey on a winding country road early one winter's morning, but as the road descends through a wooded valley, we find ourselves in the midst of thick dark fog. Visibility is reduced to a few feet; it does not seem at this moment that a drive in the countryside was such a good idea after all.

Yet soon the road climbs out of the freezing, dark valley. As we ascend the hills, we find ourselves driving in the bright sunshine once again. Cows graze in open fields. Birds sing cheerfully with eager expectation at the promise of spring.

We passed through the valley; we did not stay there.

We pass through our troubles; we do not stay in their midst forever.

A. M.

He went up on the mountain and called to Him those He Himself wanted. And they came to Him.

Mark 3:13

God, who is rich in mercy, because of His great love with which He loved us ... made us alive together with Christ.

Ephesians 2:4–5

With infinite love and compassion our Lord understood the human predicament. He had deep empathy with people; he saw their needs, their weaknesses, their desires, and their hurt. He understood and was concerned for people. Every word he spoke was uttered because he saw a need for that word in some human life. His concern was always to uplift and never to tear down, to heal and never hurt, to save and not condemn.

Charles L. Allen

God will never leave thee,
 All thy wants He knows,
Feels the pains that grieve thee,
 Sees thy cares and woes.
When in grief we languish,
 He will dry the tear,
Who His children's anguish
 Soothes with succour near.

H. S. Oswald

God loves you as though you are the only person in the world, and he loves everyone the way He loves you.

Augustine of Hippo

He calls his own sheep by name and leads them out.

John 10:3

What an incomprehensible thought: The Lord of the universe tells us, "I know you well and you are special to me. I know you by name."[1]

[1]*Exodus 33:17 MSG*

The sun, which has all those planets revolving around it, is able to ripen the smallest bunch of grapes as though it had nothing else to do in the universe.

Galileo Galilei

There is not one life which the Life-Giver ever loses out of his sight; not one which sins so that he casts it away; not one which is not so near to him that whatever touches it touches him with sorrow or with joy.

Phillips Brooks

Sweet is the solace of Thy love,
My Heavenly Friend, to me,
While through the hidden way of faith
I journey home with Thee,
Learning by quiet thankfulness
As a dear child to be.

Anna Laetitia Waring

O give thanks to the Lord of lords, for his steadfast love endures for ever.

Psalm 136:3 RSV

Abide in Me, and I in you.

As the branch cannot bear fruit of itself, unless it abides in the vine, neither can you, unless you abide in Me. I am the vine, you are the branches. He who abides in Me, and I in him, bears much fruit; for without Me you can do nothing.

John 15:4–5

If I only possessed the grace, good Jesus, to be utterly at one with you! Amidst all the variety of worldly things around me, Lord, the only thing I crave is unity with you. You are all my soul needs.

Unite, dear Friend of my heart, this unique little soul of mine to your perfect goodness. You are all mine; when shall I be yours?

Lord Jesus, my beloved, be the magnet of my heart; clasp, press, unite me forever to your sacred heart. You have made me for yourself; make me one with you. Absorb this tiny drop of life into the ocean of goodness whence it came.

Francis de Sales

Seek peace and pursue it.

Psalm 34:14

All men desire peace, but very few desire those things that make for peace.

Thomas à Kempis

Peace is not a relationship of nations. It is a condition of mind brought about by a serenity of soul. Peace is not merely an absence of war. It is also a state of mind. Lasting peace can come only to peaceful people.

Jawaharlal Nehru

All works of love are works of peace. ... Peace begins with a smile.

Mother Teresa

We look forward to the time when the power of love will replace the love of power. Then will our world know the blessings of peace.

William E. Gladstone

Christ is the fountain of peace and life.

Tobias Crisp

Live in peace; and the God of love and peace will be with you.

2 Corinthians 13:11

**Oh, that I had wings like a dove!
I would fly away and be at rest.**

Psalm 55:6

...Because so many people were coming and going that they did not even have a chance to eat, he said to them, 'Come with me by yourselves to a quiet place and get some rest.' So they went away by themselves in a boat to a solitary place.

Mark 6:31–32

Recreation is not the highest kind of enjoyment; but in its time and place it is quite as proper as prayer.

St. Irenaeus

"Come unto Me, ye weary,
    and I will give you rest."
O blessed voice of Jesus,
    which comes to hearts oppressed!
It tells of benediction,
    of pardon, grace and peace,
Of joy that hath no ending,
    of love which cannot cease.

William C. Dix

By your patience possess your souls.

Luke 21:19

Who knows whether Abraham foresaw the difficulties he would face on his faith journey: famine[1], family troubles,[2] and battles,[3] amongst others. Did Moses anticipate the troubled wilderness journey after crossing the Red Sea with the Israelites?[4] Jesus' disciples didn't always have an easy time of things either. Yet events showed that these people carried on regardless, helping create the foundation for the faith we follow.

A. M. [1]Genesis 12:10. [2]Genesis 13:7–8. [3]Genesis 14:14–16. [4]Exodus 16:3.

Never think that God's delays are God's denials. Hold on; hold fast; hold out. Patience is genius.

Georges Louis Buffon

Through the dark and stormy night
Faith beholds a feeble light
Up the blackness streaking;
Knowing God's own time is best,
In a patient hope I rest
    For the full day-breaking!

John Greenleaf Whittier

The testing of your faith produces patience.

James 1:3

Blessings of heaven above,
Blessings of the deep that lies beneath.

Genesis 49:25

A woman spent most of her life yearning impatiently for heaven. The years went slowly by, until in due time she passed from this life.

Upon her arrival in the next world, an angel took her on a tour. During the guided visit she was shown magnificent mountains, sparkling rivers, lush green fields, meadows of flowers, rolling hills and rich green woodland. Leaves rustled as tall trees swayed in the gentle breeze. Vista after vista of untold beauty unfolded, accompanied by the sounds of children laughing, of birds singing, of music that stirred the soul.

Joy filled her heart until she exclaimed, "This is tremendous! Heaven is all I ever dreamed of and more!" But the angel softly replied, "No. This is the world which you lived in, but never saw."

Retold

Praise the LORD from the earth,
Fire and hail, snow and clouds;
Stormy wind, fulfilling His word;
Mountains and all hills;
Fruitful trees and all cedars;
Beasts and all cattle;
Creeping things and flying fowl.

Psalm 148:7–10

Our Father in heaven,
Hallowed be Your name.

Your kingdom come.
Your will be done
On earth as it is in heaven.
Give us this day our daily bread.
And forgive us our debts,
As we forgive our debtors.
And do not lead us into temptation,
But deliver us from the evil one.
For Yours is the kingdom
and the power and the glory forever. Amen.

Matthew 6:9–13

What deep mysteries, my dearest brothers, are contained in the Lord's Prayer! How many and great they are! They are expressed in a few words but they are rich in spiritual powers so that nothing is left out; every petition and prayer we have to make is included. It is a compendium of heavenly doctrine.

Cyprian of Carthage

Whatever else we say when we pray, if we pray as we should, we are only saying what is already contained in the Lord's Prayer.

Augustine of Hippo

Nothing separates us from the love of God

I am persuaded that neither death nor life, nor angels nor principalities nor powers, nor things present nor things to come, nor height nor depth, nor any other created thing, shall be able to separate us from the love of God which is in Christ Jesus our Lord.

Romans 8:38–39

You are holy, Lord, the only God,
   And your deeds are wonderful.
You are love, you are wisdom.
You are humility, you are endurance.
You are rest, you are peace.
You are joy and gladness.
You are all our riches,
   and you suffice for us.

You are beauty, you are gentleness.
You are our protector,
You are our guardian and defender.
You are courage,
You are our haven and hope.
You are our faith, our great consolation.

You are our eternal life,
   great and wonderful Lord,
God almighty, merciful Saviour.

Francis of Assisi, adapted

A little while with Jesus

Jesus withdrew with His disciples to the sea. He Himself often withdrew into the wilderness and prayed.

Mark 3:7; Luke 5:16

God in his peace spreads peace all around. To behold him at rest is to rest. You see the King, so to speak, after the day-long pleadings of all the various causes upon earth, the crowds dismissed, withdrawing from all cares, seeking his rest for the night, entering his chamber with the few, whom he counts worthy of his privacy and familiarity, resting more completely as in his own retiring-place, serener of aspect, as only looking on those whom he loves.

If any of you have been rapt and hidden in this secret sanctuary of God, so that no sense of want, no pricking care, no gnawing sin, nor, which are yet more difficult to put away, any thronging phantasms of earthly images, could at all distract or disturb you, then may you glory and say, "The King has brought me into his chamber."

Bernard of Clairvaux

A little while with Jesus,
   oh, how it soothes the soul,
And gathers all the threads of life
   into a perfect whole.

Author unknown

How on a rock they stand,
Who watch His eye,
and hold His guiding hand!

J. Keble

Those who trust in the Lord are like Mount Zion, which cannot be moved, but abides forever. As the mountains surround Jerusalem, so the Lord surrounds His people from this time forth and forever.

Psalm 125:1–2

That is the way to be immovable in the midst of troubles, as a rock amidst the waves. When God is in the midst of a kingdom or city, He makes it firm as Mount Sion, that cannot be removed. When He is in the midst of a soul, though calamities throng about it on all hands, and roar like the billows of the sea, yet there is a constant calm within, such a peace as the world can neither give nor take away.

Robert Leighton

You have given me the shield
of Your salvation;
Your right hand has held me up,
Your gentleness has made me great.
You enlarged my path under me,
So my feet did not slip.

Psalm 18:35–36

Receive, please, instruction from His mouth, and lay up His words in your heart.

Job 22:22

The Bible is God's chart for you to steer by, to keep you from the bottom of the sea, and to show you where the harbour is, and how to reach it without running on rocks and bars.

Henry Ward Beecher

The Bible is the greatest traveller in the world. It penetrates to every country. It is seen in the royal place and in the humble cottage. It is the friend of emperors and beggars. It is read by the light of the dim candle amid Arctic snows. It is read under the glare of the equatorial sun. It is read in city and country, amid the crowds and in solitude. Wherever the message is received, it frees the mind from bondage and fills the heart with gladness.

Arthur Tappan Pierson

Your word is a lamp to my feet and a light to my path.

Psalm 119:105

Whatever you want men to do to you, do also to them.

Matthew 7:12

Love has a thousand varied notes to move the human heart.

George Crabbe

I expect to pass through this world but once. Any good thing therefore that I can do, or any kindness that I can show to any fellow-creature, let me do it now; let me not defer or neglect it, for I shall not pass this way again.

Stephen Grellet

Is life not full of opportunities for learning Love? Every man and woman every day has a thousand of them. The world is not a playground; it is a schoolroom. Life is not a holiday, but an education. And the one eternal lesson for us all is *how better we can love*. ... To love abundantly, and to love forever is to live forever.

Henry Drummond

The spirit of a person's life is ever shedding some power, just as a flower is steadily bestowing fragrance upon the air.

Thomas Starr King

If we love one another, God abides in us, and His love has been perfected in us.

1 John 4:12

Wisdom is with aged men,
And with length of days, understanding.

Job 12:12

A man's age is something impressive; it sums up his life: maturity reached slowly and against many obstacles, illnesses cured, griefs and despairs overcome, and unconscious risks taken; maturity formed through so many desires, hopes, regrets, forgotten things, loves. A man's age represents a fine cargo of experiences and memories.

Antoine de Saint-Exupéry

Age is opportunity no less
Than youth itself, though in another dress;
And as the evening twilight fades away,
The sky is filled with stars, invisible by day.

Henry Wadsworth Longfellow

Those who love deeply never grow old; they may die of old age, but they die young.

Arthur Wing Pinero

I have created you and cared for you since you were born. I will be your God through all your lifetime, Yes, even when your hair is white with age. I made you and I will care for you.

Isaiah 46:3–4 TLB

Unto You I lift up my eyes,
O You who dwell in the heavens.

Psalm 123:1

In the eye of the hurricane, there is peace.

Author unknown

In perplexities – when we cannot tell what to do, when we cannot understand what is going on around us – let us be calmed and steadied and made patient by the thought that what is hidden from us is not hidden from Him.

Frances Ridley Havergal

Dear Lord, sometimes I feel like the storms of life are overwhelming me, yet You promise I can find a refuge in You. You are the Saviour of my today and my eternity. I ask you to help me to grow in faith, that I may be secure in the knowledge that there is never a moment when I am not overshadowed by your love.

Blessed quietness, holy quietness,
Blest assurance in my soul!
On the stormy sea, Jesus speaks to me,
And the billows cease to roll.

Manie P. Ferguson

My value

A motivational speaker started his seminar by holding up a £20 note. In the room of 200, he asked, "Who would like this £20 note?" Hands started going up.

He said, "I am going to give this £20 to one of you, but first, let me do this." He proceeded to crumple the bill.

He then asked, "Who still wants it?" Still the hands were up in the air.

"Well," he replied, "what if I do this?" And he dropped it on the ground and started to grind it into the floor with his shoe. He picked it up, now crumpled and dirty. "Now who still wants it?" Still the hands went into the air.

"My friends, you have all learned a very valuable lesson. No matter what I did to the money, you still wanted it because it did not decrease in value. It is still worth £20.

"Many times in our lives, we are crumpled, dropped and ground into the dirt by the decisions we make and the circumstances that come our way. We feel as though we are worthless. But no matter what has happened or what will happen, you will never lose your value in God's eyes. To him, dirty or clean, crumpled or finely creased, you are still priceless."

Author unknown

O Lord, make of me an instrument of your peace.

Where there is hatred, let me sow love;
Where there is doubt, let me sow faith;
Where there is injury, let me sow pardon;
Where there is discord, let me sow unity;
Where there is error, let me sow the truth;
Where there is despair, let me sow hope;
Where there is sadness, let me sow joy;
Where there is darkness,
   let me sow the light.

O Lord, make of me an instrument
   of your peace.

O Master, that I may not seek
To be consoled, but to console;
Not to be understood, but to understand;
Not to be loved, but rather to love;
For it is in giving that we will receive;
And in forsaking that we truly gain;
By forgiving, that we are forgiven;
And in dying,
   that we are born again to eternal life.

Author unknown, often attributed to Francis of Assisi

He has put in his heart
the ability to teach.

Exodus 35:34

A teacher affects eternity; he can never tell where his influence stops.

Henry Brooks Adams

The art of teaching is the art of assisting discovery.

Author unknown

If we work marble, it will perish; if we work upon brass, time will efface it; if we rear temples, they will crumble into dust; but if we work upon immortal minds and instill into them just principles, we are then engraving that upon tables which no time will efface, but will brighten and brighten to all eternity.

Daniel Webster

These words which I command you today shall be in your heart. You shall teach them diligently to your children, and shall talk of them when you sit in your house, when you walk by the way, when you lie down, and when you rise up.

Deuteronomy 6:6–7

**Dear God, be good to me;
the sea is so large,
and my boat is so small.**

Traditional prayer of a Breton fisherman

That rushing flood I had no strength to meet,
No power to flee: my present, future, past,
My self, my sorrow, and my sin I cast
In utter helplessness at Jesu's feet;
Then bent me to the storm, if such His will.
He saw the winds and waves,
        and whispered, 'Peace, be still.'

And there was calm! O Saviour, I have proved
That Thou to help and save art *really* near!
How else this quiet rest from grief, and fear,
And all distress? The cross is not removed;
I must go forth to bear it as before,
But, leaning on Thine arm,
        I dread its weight no more.

Frances Ridley Havergal

I, the LORD your God,
will hold your right hand,
Saying to you,
"Fear not, I will help you."

Isaiah 41:13

A day's strength

Have you not known?
Have you not heard?
The everlasting God, the LORD,
The Creator of the ends of the earth,
Neither faints nor is weary.
His understanding is unsearchable.
He gives power to the weak,
And to those who have no might
He increases strength.

Even the youths shall faint and be weary,
And the young men shall utterly fall,
But those who wait on the LORD
Shall renew their strength;
They shall mount up with wings like eagles,
They shall run and not be weary,
They shall walk and not faint.

Isaiah 40:28–31

The day returns and brings us the petty round of irritating concerns and duties. Help us to play the man, help us to perform them with laughter and kind faces; let cheerfulness abound with industry.

Give us to go blithely on our business all this day, bring us to our resting beds weary and content, and grant us in the end the gift of sleep.

Robert Louis Stevenson

The book of books, the storehouse, and magazine of life and comfort, the Holy Scriptures.

George Herbert

He said to them, "Therefore every scribe instructed concerning the kingdom of heaven is like a householder who brings out of his treasure things new and old."

Matthew 13:52

The highest earthly enjoyments are but a shadow of the joy I find in reading God's word.

Lady Jane Grey

I have found in the Bible words for my inmost thoughts, songs for my joy, utterances for my hidden griefs and pleadings for my shame and feebleness.

Samuel Taylor Coleridge

The Bible is a window in this prison-world, through which we may look into eternity.

Timothy Dwight

Thanks be to the Gospel, by means of which we also, who did not see Christ when he came into this world, seem to be with him when we read his deeds.

Ambrose

Though I walk in the midst of trouble, You will revive me.

Psalm 138:7

Our life is full of brokenness - broken relationships, broken promises, broken expectations. How can we live with that brokenness without becoming bitter and resentful except by returning again and again to God's faithful presence in our lives.

Henri Nouwen

I journey through a desert
drear and wild,
Yet is my heart by such
sweet thoughts beguiled,
Of him on whom I lean,
my strength, my stay,
I can forget the sorrows of the way.

Author unknown

A rule I have had for years is: to treat the Lord Jesus Christ as a personal friend. His is not a creed, a mere doctrine, but it is he himself we have.

Dwight L. Moody

Grace to you and peace from God our Father and the Lord Jesus Christ.

Romans 1:7

I will go in the strength of the Lord GOD.

Psalm 71:16

The story has often been retold: A father watches as his child struggles to lift a heavy object.

"You're not using all your strength," he remarks gently.

"But I'm doing the best I can!" insists his son.

"Not quite. You haven't asked me to help you," replies his father.

How frequently we struggle with the heavy burdens of life, when our Father stands by, willing and ready to help lift the load.

A. M.

He that takes his cares on himself loads himself in vain with an uneasy burden. I will cast my cares on God; he has bidden me; they cannot burden him.

Joseph Hall

Give me a task too big,
Too hard for human hands.
Then shall I come at length
To lean on You;
And leaning, find my strength.

Wilbur Humphrey Fowler

Then David danced before the LORD with all his might.

2 Samuel 6:14

Oh come, let us sing to the LORD!
Let us shout joyfully
   to the Rock of our salvation.
Let us come before His presence
   with thanksgiving;
Let us shout joyfully to Him with psalms.

Psalm 95:1–2

Confident swimmers are happiest in the water. Liberated from the gravity of an earth-bound existence, they revel in the near weightlessness. When we're trusting in God, we are freer, less weighed down with the concerns of our daily lives, because we are letting Him buoy us up. "Therefore if the Son makes you free, you shall be free indeed."[1] That freedom comes when we place ourselves in His care, know He's holding us.

A. M. [1]*John 8:36*

Eternal God, the light of the minds that know you, the joy of the hearts that love you and the strength of the wills that serve you, grant us so to know you, that we may truly love you, and so to love you that we may fully serve you, whom to serve is perfect freedom.

St Augustine of Hippo

Out of weakness made strong.

Hebrews 11:34

The things we try to avoid and fight against — tribulation, suffering and persecution—are the very things that produce abundant joy in us. Huge waves that would frighten the ordinary swimmer produce a tremendous thrill for the surfer who has ridden them. "We are more than conquerors through Him" in all these things—not in spite of them, but in the midst of them. A saint doesn't know the joy of the Lord in spite of tribulation, but because of it.

Oswald Chambers

Troubles are often the tools by which God fashions us for better things.

Henry Ward Beecher

No test or temptation that comes your way is beyond the course of what others have had to face. All you need to remember is that God will never let you down; he'll never let you be pushed past your limit; he'll always be there to help you come through it.

1 Corinthians 10:13 MSG

Keep yourselves in the love of God, looking for the mercy of our Lord Jesus Christ unto eternal life.

Jude 21

Then Jesus, moved with compassion, stretched out His hand and touched him, and said to him, "I am willing; be cleansed."

Mark 1:41

The Lord is my shepherd.[1] Not was, not may be, nor will be. The Lord *is* my shepherd. He is on Sunday, is on Monday, and is through every day of the week; is in January, is in December, and every month of the year; is at home, and is in China; is in peace, and is in war; in abundance, and in penury.

James Hudson Taylor

[1]*Psalm 23:1*

I looked to Jesus, and I found
In him my star, my sun;
And in that light of life I'll walk
Till travelling days are done.

Author unknown

We have heard his voice.

Surely the Lord our God has shown us His glory and His greatness, and we have heard His voice. We have seen this day that God speaks with man; yet he still lives.

Deuteronomy 5:24

If you would speak or hear of God aright, leave the body and your bodily senses, quit earth, quit sea, set air beneath you, outstrip the boundaries of time, the ordinances of the seasons, outsoar the stars, and all their wonders, their order, their harmony, their splendour, their relations and their motions. Overpass all with your mind.

Pass on! Let your mind mount up above every creature. Exalting your spirit higher still, consider the Divine Nature abiding, unalterable, unchangeable, impassable, simple, uncompounded, indivisible, light inaccessible, power unspeakable, greatness illimitable, glory exceeding, goodness most amiable, beauty inconceivable, enrapturing with mighty strength the wounded soul, but which words are inadequate even to shadow forth. There is the Father, the Son and the Holy Spirit, the Nature uncreate, the Royal Majesty, the substantial Goodness.

Basil of Caesarea, adapted

Mercy triumphs over judgment.

James 2:13

Among the attributes of God, although they are all equal, mercy shines with even more brilliancy than justice.

Miguel de Cervantes

Justice is getting what we deserve. Mercy is another matter.

There is a story of a woman who came before Napoleon begging the pardon of her son. It was his second offence, and according to justice, the penalty was death. "I don't ask for justice," said the mother, "I plead for mercy." "But," said the emperor, "he does not deserve mercy." "Sir," cried the mother, "it would not be mercy if he deserved it, and mercy is all I ask." "Well, then," said the emperor, "I will have mercy."

Her son was saved.

Retold

Have mercy upon me, O God,
According to Your lovingkindness;
According to the multitude
of Your tender mercies,
Blot out my transgressions.
I have trusted in Your mercy;
My heart shall rejoice in Your salvation.

Psalm 51:1; 13:5

My presence shall go with you,
and I will give you rest.

Exodus 33:14

In all their affliction He was afflicted, and the Angel of His Presence saved them; in His love and in His pity He redeemed them; and He bore them and carried them all the days of old.

Isaiah 63:9

Think back to yesterday. Before your day even started, Jesus was with you as you slept, watching over you. Morning came, and just as sure as the sun rose, he was there. When you thought about the day ahead, he was there, just waiting for you to ask his help in planning and carrying out that plan. On your way to work, he was right beside you.

Every time you encountered a problem, he was waiting with the answer you needed, hoping you would ask him for it. When you heard some good news, he was happy along with you. When the day took a difficult turn, he was there to comfort you.

Today is a new day. Just as he was there beside you yesterday, he is with you now.

A. M.

Through love serve one another.

Galatians 5:13

A loving heart is the beginning of all knowledge.

Thomas Carlyle

Flowers leave some of their fragrance in the hand that bestows them.

Chinese proverb

Have you had a kindness shown?
Pass it on;
'Twas not given for thee alone,
Pass it on;
Let it travel down the years,
Let it wipe another's tears,
'Til in Heaven the deed appears—
Pass it on.

Henry Burton

Everybody can be great … because anybody can serve. You don't have to have a college degree to serve. You don't have to make your subject and verb agree to serve. You only need a heart full of grace. A soul generated by love.

Martin Luther King Jr.

My beloved friends, let us continue to love each other since love comes from God. Everyone who loves is born of God and experiences a relationship with God.

1 John 4:7 MSG

Answer me speedily, O Lord;
My spirit fails!

Psalm 143:7

"Help me," cried the desperate mother on behalf of her daughter, whom Jesus then healed.[1]

"Save us, O God of our salvation," cried the people, and He did.[2]

"Heal me, O Lord, and I shall be healed; Save me, and I shall be saved," declared Jeremiah the prophet who, despite his many troubles, lived a long and productive life.[3]

"Have mercy on me," cried a blind man to Jesus. Minutes later, he received his sight.[4]

"Help me, O Lord my God! Oh, save me according to Your mercy," pleaded David, the man raised from the sheepfold to the throne.[5]

One central feature of these few examples is that each person, in their own way, called on God to help them.

"Call upon Me in the day of trouble," God tells us, but He doesn't leave it there: "I will deliver you."[6]

A. M. [1]Matthew 15:22–28; [2]1 Chronicles 16:35; [3]Jeremiah 17:14; [4]Mark 10:47–52; [5]Psalm 109:26; [6]Psalm 50:15

Therefore I will look to the Lord; I will wait for the God of my salvation; My God will hear me.

Micah 7:7

Every day is a gift I receive from heaven; let us enjoy today that which it bestows.

Marie de Mancroix

Although we may need to make practical preparations for the future, we should not carry such preparations as weights, lest they turn into worries. "Be anxious for nothing,"[1] the Bible teaches.

[1]*Philippians 4:6*

Let us then think only of the present, and not even permit our minds to wander with curiosity into the future. This future is not yet ours; perhaps it never will be. It is exposing ourselves to temptation to wish to anticipate God, and to prepare ourselves for things which he may not destine for us. If such things should come to pass, he will give us light and strength according to the need. Let us give heed to the present, whose duties are pressing; it is fidelity to the present which prepares us for fidelity in the future.

François de la Mothe-Fénelon

May the Lord make you increase and abound in love to one another and to all.

1 Thessalonians 3:12

Loving-kindness is twice blessed; it blesses him who gives and him who receives.

Author unknown

By cultivating the beautiful we scatter the seeds of heavenly flowers, as by doing good we cultivate those that belong to humanity.

John Howard

If I can put one touch of a rosy sunset into the life of any man or woman, I shall feel that I have worked with God.

George MacDonald

Be kind to one another, tenderhearted, forgiving one another, just as God in Christ forgave you.

Ephesians 4:32

Do right, and God's recompense to you will be the power of doing more right. Give, and God's reward to you will be the spirit of giving more: a blessed spirit, for it is the Spirit of God himself, whose Life is the blessedness of giving. Love, and God will pay you with the capacity of more love; for love is Heaven—love is God within you.

Frederick William Robertson

Have you journeyed
to the springs of the sea
or walked in the recesses of the deep?

Job 38:16

Move my heart with the calm, smooth flow of your grace. Let the river of your love run through my soul. May my soul be carried by the current of your love towards the wide, infinite ocean of heaven.

Stretch out my heart with your strength, as you stretch out the sky above the earth. Smooth out any wrinkles of hatred or resentment. Enlarge my soul that it may know more fully your truth.

Gilbert of Hoyland

How priceless is your unfailing love! Both high and low among men find refuge in the shadow of your wings. They feast on the abundance of your house; you give them drink from your river of delights. For with you is the fountain of life.

Psalm 36:7–9 NIV

Seek the LORD and His strength;
Seek His face evermore.

1 Chronicles 16:11

Prayer is the wing wherewith the soul flies to heaven, and meditation the eye wherewith we see God.

Ambrose

All the troubles of life come upon us because we refuse to sit quietly for a while each day in our room.

Blaise Pascal

Prayer is a haven to the shipwrecked man, an anchor to them that are sinking in the waves, a staff to the limbs that totter, a mine of jewels to the poor, a healer of diseases and a guardian of health.

John Chrysostom

Lord Jesus Christ, you said that you are the Way, the Truth, and the Life;[1] let us never stray from you, who are the Way; nor distrust you, who are the Truth; nor rest in any other but you, who are the Life, beyond whom there is nothing to be desired, either in heaven or on earth. We ask it for your name's sake.

Desiderius Erasmus. [1]*John 14:6*

The goodness of God endures continually.

Psalm 52:1

You in Your mercy have led forth
The people whom You have redeemed;
You have guided them in Your strength
To Your holy habitation.

Exodus 15:13

There is but one way to tranquillity of mind and happiness, and that is to account no external things your own, but to commit all to God.

Epictetus

God is a guest that requires the upper rooms, that is, the head and the heart.

Edmund Calamy

As a little child relies
On a care beyond his own;
Knows he's neither strong nor wise,
Fears to stir a step alone:
Let me thus with Thee abide,
As my Father, Guard, and Guide.

John Newton

Bless the LORD, O my soul,
And forget not all His benefits.

Psalm 103:2

If one should give me a dish of sand, and tell me there were particles of iron in it, I might look for them with my eyes, and search for them with my clumsy fingers, and be unable to detect them; but let me take a magnet and sweep through it, and how would it draw to itself the almost invisible particles by the mere power of attraction.

The unthankful heart, like my finger in the sand, discovers no mercies; but let the thankful heart sweep through the day, and as the magnet finds the iron, so it will find, in every hour, some heavenly blessings, only the iron in God's sand is gold!

Henry Ward Beecher

The worship most acceptable to God comes from a thankful and cheerful heart.

Plutarch

Being justified by faith, we have peace with God through our Lord Jesus Christ.

Romans 5:1

A person may go to heaven without health, without riches, without honours, without learning, without friends; but he can never go there without Christ.

John Dyer

Ah, Christians, ring the bells of your hearts, tire the salute of your most joyous songs, "For unto us a child is born, unto us a Son is given."[1] Dance, O my heart, and ring out peals of gladness! Ye drops of blood within my veins dance every one of you! Oh! All my nerves become harp strings, and let gratitude touch you with angelic fingers! And thou, my tongue, shout—shout to his praise who hath said to thee—"Unto thee a child is born, unto thee a Son is given."

Charles Haddon Spurgeon. [1] *Isaiah 9:6*

Blessed be the God and Father of our Lord Jesus Christ, who has blessed us with every spiritual blessing in the heavenly places in Christ.

Ephesians 1:3

Better is a little with the fear of the LORD,
Than great treasure with trouble.

Proverbs 15:16

Wealth is like a viper, which is harmless if you know how to take hold of it; but, if you do not, it will twine round your hand and bite you.

Clement of Alexandria

"Simplicity is a very rare thing in our age" was perhaps surprisingly spoken not in the twenty-first century, but in the first, by Publius Ovidius Naso, better known as Ovid.

A. M.

Grant me, O Lord,
to know what is worth knowing,
to love what is worth loving,
to praise what delights you most,
to value what is precious to you,
and to reject whatever is evil in your eyes.
Give me true discernment,
so that I may judge rightly
between things that differ.
Above all, may I search out and do
what is pleasing to you;
through Jesus Christ my Lord.

Thomas à Kempis

While the earth remains

Seedtime and harvest,
Cold and heat,
Winter and summer,
And day and night
Shall not cease.

Genesis 8:22

This most generous God who gives seed to the farmer that becomes bread for your meals is more than extravagant with you. He gives you something you can then give away, which grows into full-formed lives, robust in God, wealthy in every way, so that you can be generous in every way, producing with us great praise to God.

2 Corinthians 2:9–11 MSG

Because I have been given much,
I, too, must give:
Because of Thy great bounty, Lord,
Each day I live
I shall divide my gifts from Thee
With every brother that I see
Who has the need of help from me.

Grace Noll Crowell

We are born for love. It is the principle of existence, and its only end.

Benjamin Disraeli

We should not live to please ourselves. Each of us should live to please his neighbor.

Romans 15:1–2 NLV

Let us not love with words or tongue but with actions and in truth.

1 John 3:18 NIV

Be supportive. Share each other's burdens

Galatians 6:2 NLT

Love is just a word until someone comes along and gives it meaning.

Author unknown

Familiar acts are beautiful through love.

Percy Bysshe Shelley

The vocation of every man and woman is to serve other people.

Leo Tolstoy

Impart unto me, O God, I pray Thee, the spirit of Thy love, that I may be more anxious to give than to receive, more eager to understand than to be understood, more thoughtful for others, more forgetful of myself.

F. B. Meyer

[Daniel] kneeled upon his knees three times a day, and prayed, and gave thanks before his God.

Daniel 6:10

We are told that Daniel, the Hebrew captive who became advisor to the Babylonian king, stopped to pray three times a day. Surely if Daniel could do this, as busy as he was, with as many responsibilities as he held, and with as many crises as he faced, we should likewise make time for God each day.

A. M.

A Christian will find his parenthesis for prayer, even through his busiest hours.

Richard Cecil

Lord, help me today to realise that you will be speaking to me through the events of the day, through people, through things, and through all creation.

Give me ears, eyes and heart to perceive you, however veiled your presence may be.

Give me insight to see through the exterior of things to the interior truth. Give me your spirit of discernment.

O Lord, you know how busy I must be this day. If I forget you, do not forget me.

Jacob Astley, before the battle of Edgehill, 1642

**If we are faithless, He remains faithful;
He cannot deny Himself.**

2 Timothy 2:13

There can be no such thing as losing with God. God cannot tolerate the loss of what really belongs to him. This is a truth we cannot explain, and yet, it helps us to keep silence in the presence of some of the riddles of life.

"The Son of man is come to seek and to save that which was lost."[1] The lost sheep, and the lost piece of money, and the lost son of the parables, were only lost for a time: "I have found my sheep... I have found the piece... This my son was lost, and is found." This is a precious thought, assuring us that in all that God does, there is a meaning and a purpose. He takes care that "nothing be lost."

P. F. Eliot. [1]Matthew 18:11 KJV

Of those whom You gave Me I have lost none.

John 18:9

The gift of God is eternal life
in Christ Jesus our Lord.

Romans 6:23

There is one only calm and sure tranquillity; one only solid, firm and lasting security; and this is ours when withdrawn from the whirlwinds of this unquiet life, and settled in the anchorage of the harbour of salvation, we lift our eyes from earth to heaven; and, admitted to the grace of the Lord, and made near to God in our mind, we rejoice.

How firm, how immovable a defence is ours! What a heavenly safeguard of unfading blessings, when we are loose from the snares of this entangling life, and purged from the dregs of earth into the light of immortality and eternity! There is no need of money, of the hand or work of man, to obtain this highest dignity and power. It is the free, gratuitous gift of God.

Robert Milman

Be merciful to me, O God, be merciful to me!
For my soul trusts in You;
And in the shadow of Your wings I will make my refuge,
Until these calamities have passed by.

Psalm 57:1

Since you were precious in My sight,
You have been honored,
And I have loved you.

Isaiah 43:4

What is precious to God? We may value possessions and wealth, but it is people, not things, that are most precious to him—so precious indeed that he calls us saints. We may not feel like saints, ever conscious of our failings, but it is our very dependence on him that makes us those "in whom he delights."[1]

A. M. [1]Psalm 16:3

The saints are God's jewels, highly esteemed by and dear to him; they are a royal diadem in his hand.

Matthew Henry

A saint is a human creature devoured and transformed by love.

Evelyn Underhill

God creates out of nothing. Wonderful, you say. Yes, to be sure, but he does what is still more wonderful: he makes saints out of sinners.

Søren Kierkegaard

The world is a book
and every step turns a new page.

Alphonse de Lamartine

A story is told of an elderly woman who slipped and fell on a busy street. Several people quickly went to assist her, but she was already struggling to hoist herself up. "I'm all right," she assured them. "I always fall forwards, never backwards."

When we've "taken a fall," instead of dwelling on the mistake or hurt, we need to make it a fall forward by learning from it and looking to the future.

A. M.

I am willing to go anywhere, anywhere, anywhere—so long as it's forward.

David Livingstone

What a God we have! And how fortunate we are to have him, this Father of our Master Jesus! Because Jesus was raised from the dead, we've been given a brand-new life and have everything to live for, including a future in heaven—and the future starts now!

1 Peter 1:3–4 MSG

Let patience have its perfect work, that you may be perfect and complete, lacking nothing.

James 1:4

Be patient with everyone, but above all, with yourself. I mean, do not be disturbed because of your imperfections, and always rise up bravely from a fall. I am glad that you make a daily new beginning; there is no better means of progress in the spiritual life than to be continually beginning afresh, and never to think that we have done enough.

Francis de Sales

It's not that I feel less weak, but Thou
Wilt be my strength; it is not that I see
Less sin; but more of pardoning love with Thee
And all-sufficient grace. Enough! And now
All fluttering thought is stilled; I only rest,
And feel that Thou art near, and know that I
am blessed.

Frances Ridley Havergal

God is a refuge for us.

Psalm 62:8

The poor and needy seek water,
   but there is none,
Their tongues fail for thirst.
I, the LORD, will hear them;
I, the God of Israel, will not forsake them.
I will open rivers in desolate heights,
And fountains in the midst of the valleys;
I will make the wilderness a pool of water,
And the dry land springs of water.

Isaiah 41:17–18

Take courage. We walk in the wilderness today
and in the Promised Land tomorrow.

L. Moody

Faith hath this privilege, never to be ashamed;
it takes sanctuary in God, and sits and sings
under the shadow of his wings.

Robert Leighton

Ever shine Thy face upon me
As I work and wait on Thee;
Resting beneath Thy smile, Lord Jesus,
Earth's dark shadows flee.

Jean Sophia Pigott

He comforts us in all our tribulation.

2 Corinthians 1:4

Prepare your minds for action; discipline yourselves; set all your hope on the grace that Jesus Christ will bring you when he is revealed.

1 Peter 1:13 NRSV

Picture the farmer. He's finished a difficult year and is fretting about the future. Will the coming year's harvest be any better? No matter his dismay, he can't just stay in the farmhouse, staring into his tea at the kitchen table. He's got to think about the future of the farm, about his family.

So he picks himself up. He goes out with trepidation, planting his seeds. Winds will blow, rain will fall, sun will shine. In time, the crops will grow. He'll come back to the farmhouse a lot happier, with the fruits of the harvest safely in his barn.

If he had not been able to visualize the results, he never would have sown the seeds. If had had never gone out, there would be no harvest. Leaving our comfort zone and stepping out on the strength of our vision, even when it is difficult, is how we'll make a difference.

A. M.

The one who goes out weeping, carrying a bag of seeds, will surely return with a joyful song, bearing sheaves from his harvest.

Psalm 126:6

In that sweet by and by
we shall meet on that beautiful shore.

Ira David Sankey

Christ has manifested most amazing love to believers, in preparing for their eternal abode, mansions of glory, a house not made with hands, eternal in the heavens; a city which has foundations, whose builder and maker is God. Heaven is a prepared place for believers; prepared by Christ in his infinite love. The love of Christ will make heaven a glorious, happy abode indeed.

Octavius Winslow

Heaven is a place where all joy is enjoyed!
In heaven, there will be:
   mirth without sadness,
   light without darkness,
   sweetness without bitterness,
   life without death,
   rest without labour,
   plenty without poverty!
Oh, what joy enters into the believer—when the believer enters into the joy of his Lord!

William Dyer

His lord said to him, "Well done, good and faithful servant; you were faithful over a few things, I will make you ruler over many things. Enter into the joy of your lord."

Matthew 25:21

Do not worry about your life.

Matthew 6:25

I will give peace and quietness. I will not leave you comfortless: I will come to you. My people will dwell in a peaceful habitation, in secure dwellings, and in quiet resting places.

Fear not, for I am with you; be not dismayed, for I am your God. I will strengthen you, yes, I will help you, I will uphold you with My righteous right hand.

1 Chronicles 22:9; John 14:18 KJV, Isaiah 32:18, Isaiah 41:10

If the basis of peace is God, the secret of peace is trust.

J. N. Figgis

I bless thee for thy peace, O God,
 Deep as the unfathomed sea.
Which falls like sunshine on the road
 Of those who trust in thee.

Author unknown

You have promised that you will keep him in perfect peace whose mind is stayed on you. I need to focus my thoughts on you. The peace I'm seeking comes from trust in you; I won't get upset by bad news if I have my heart fixed. Help me to trust you. Amen.

Prayer based on Isaiah 26:3 and Psalm 112:7

In the hour of adversity be not without hope, for crystal rain falls from black clouds.

Persian proverb

No matter the depth of our troubles, there still shines a ray of hope, because the Lord is a present help in time of trouble.[1] No matter the heartbreak and loss, God is near.[2] The tears may flow, yet comfort is promised for those who mourn.[3] When we walk through darkest valley, we are not alone, for He is with us.[4]

A. M. [1]Psalm 46:1, [2]Psalm 34:18, [3]Matthew 5:4, [4]Psalm 23:4

As the deep blue of Heaven
    brightens into stars,
So God's great love
    shines forth in promises,
Which, falling softly
    through our prison bars,
Daze not our eyes,
    but with their soft light bless.
Ladders of light God sets against the skies,
Upon whose golden rungs
    we step by step arise.
Until we tread the halls of Paradise.

E. H.

Our light affliction, which is but for a moment, is working for us a far more exceeding and eternal weight of glory.

2 Corinthians 4:17

No one is useless in this world who lightens the burden of it for anyone else.

Charles Dickens

Give, and it will be given to you: good measure, pressed down, shaken together, and running over will be put into your bosom. For with the same measure that you use, it will be measured back to you.

Luke 6:38

Make it a rule ... never, if possible, to lie down at night without being able to say, "I have made one human being at least a little wiser, a little happier, or a little better this day."

Charles Kingsley

Look up and not down; look forward and not back; look out and not in; and lend a hand.

Edward Everett Hale

Kindness in words creates confidence. Kindness in thinking creates profoundness. Kindness in giving creates love.

Lao-tzu

The door to happiness swings outward.

Søren Kierkegaard

Rest in the LORD,
and wait patiently for Him.

Psalm 37:7

Rest time is not waste time. It is economy to gather fresh strength... It is wisdom to take occasional furlough. In the long run, we shall do more by sometimes doing less.

Charles H. Spurgeon

Once I knew what it was to rest upon the rock of God's promises, and it was indeed a precious resting place, but now I rest in His grace. He is teaching me that the bosom of His love is a far sweeter resting-place than even the rock of His promises.

Hannah Whitall Smith

Was there ever kinder shepherd
Half so gentle, half so sweet,
As the Savior who would have us
Come and gather at His feet?

Frederick W. Faber

I am like an olive tree flourishing in the house of God; I trust in God's unfailing love for ever and ever.

Psalm 52:8

I heard the voice of the Lord.

Isaiah 6:8

The LORD passed by, and a great and strong wind tore into the mountains and broke the rocks in pieces before the LORD, but the LORD was not in the wind; and after the wind an earthquake, but the LORD was not in the earthquake; and after the earthquake a fire, but the LORD was not in the fire; and after the fire a still small voice.

1 Kings 19:11–12

Quietness is the still point of the turning world.

T. S. Eliot

It seems that God speaks mostly in small, quiet ways. If we do not cease our busy activities, we might not notice. If we do not still ourselves, we may not hear. But when we pause momentarily, close our eyes to the outside world, take a slow deep breath, suddenly we are aware. He is here.

A. M.

For those who look with their physical eyes,
God is nowhere to be seen.
For those who contemplate Him in spirit,
He is everywhere.
He is in all, yet beyond all.

St Symeon

When [the shepherd] brings out his own sheep, he goes before them; and the sheep follow him, for they know his voice.

John 10:4

Run the straight race through
God's good grace,
Lift up thine eyes, and seek his face;
Life with its way before us lies,
Christ is the path, and Christ the prize.

Cast care aside, upon thy Guide
Lean, and his mercy will provide;
Lean, and the trusting soul shall prove
Christ is its life, and Christ its love.

Faint not nor fear, his arms are near,
He changeth not, and thou art dear;
Only believe, and thou shalt see
That Christ is all in all to thee.

John Samuel Bewley Monsell

The more the soul looks upon Christ, the more it loves; and still, the more it loves, the more it delights to look upon him.

Robert Leighton

Put your trust in the Lord.

Psalm 4:5

Be happy in a moment, that's enough. Each moment is all we need, no more.

Mother Teresa

Live in peace without worrying about the future. Unnecessary worrying and imagining the worst possible scenario will strangle your faith. ... The future is not yet yours—perhaps it never will be. And when tomorrow comes it will probably be different from what you had imagined. ... Above all, live in the present moment and God will give you all the grace you need.

François de la Mothe-Fénelon

Anticipated sorrows are harder to bear than real ones, because Christ does not support us under them.

Edward Payson

Now to him who is able to keep [you] from stumbling, and to present you faultless before the presence of his glory in great joy, to God our Saviour, who alone is wise, be glory and majesty, dominion and power, both now and forever. Amen.

Jude 24–25 (WEB)

**Let my mouth be filled with your praise
And with your glory all the day.**

Blessed are the people
   who know the joyful sound!
They walk, O Lord,
   in the light of your countenance.

In your name they rejoice all day long,
And in your righteousness they are exalted.
For you are the glory of their strength.
I will hope continually,
And will praise you yet more and more.

My mouth shall tell of your righteousness
And your salvation all the day,
For I do not know their limits.

My lips shall greatly rejoice
   when I sing to you,
And my soul, which you have redeemed.

I give thanks to you, O God, I give thanks!
For your wondrous works
declare that your name is near.

Based on Psalm 71:8; 89:15–17; 71:14–15, 23; 75:1

It is no longer I who live, but Christ lives in me.

Galatians 2:20

Take heed, dear friends, to the promptings of love and truth in your hearts. Trust them as the leadings of God whose Light shows us our darkness and brings us to new life. Bring the whole of your life under the ordering of the spirit of Christ. Are you open to the healing power of God's love? Cherish that which is of God within you, so that this love may grow in you and guide you. Let your worship and your daily life enrich each other. Treasure your experience of God, however it comes to you. Remember that Christianity is not a notion but a way.

"Advice and Queries," the Society of Friends

God's thoughts, his will, his love, his judgments are all man's home. To think his thoughts, to choose his will, to love his loves, to judge his judgments, and thus to know that he is in us, is to be at home.

George MacDonald

The peace of God, which surpasses all understanding, will guard your hearts and minds through Christ Jesus.

Philippians 4:7

Jesus lay in the boat sleeping. The waves rose, the wind blew and the storm battered about the small vessel. His disciples were afraid: afraid of the wind, afraid of the waves and fearful for their lives. They came to Jesus, woke him up, begging for his help. The answer lay in his power. He said, "Peace, be still," and there was peace. The wind ceased, and there was a great calm.[1] No matter the turmoil of our life, we too can find peace if we turn to Jesus for his help.

A. M. [1]*Mark 4:35–41*

Peace, peace!
Look for its bright increase,
Deepening, widening, year by year,
Like a sunlit river, strong, calm, and clear;
Lean on His love through this earthly vale,
For His word and His work shall never fail,
And 'He is our peace.'

Frances Ridley Havergal

God is Spirit.

John 4:24

God is like the air we breathe—all around us, invisible and vital to our health and happiness. Just as we need to breathe clean, fresh air to be strong and healthy physically, we need to partake of God's Spirit to be strong and healthy spiritually. Under normal circumstances, breathing is an unconscious, involuntary act. God would like our relationship with him to be that natural, and he created us with all the necessary equipment. But unlike breathing, for most of us making that connection with God doesn't come so easily; it requires a conscious effort on our part. It is an effort that is worthwhile.

Breathe on me, breath of God,
Fill me with life anew,
That I may love what Thou dost love,
And do what Thou wouldst do.
Breathe on me, breath of God,
Blend all my soul with Thine,
Until this earthly part of me
Glows with Thy fire divine.
Breathe on me, breath of God,
So shall I never die,
But live with Thee the perfect life
Of Thine eternity.

Edwin Hatch

It is the invitation of Christ that gives you the right to approach him.

William Howells

The two disciples heard [John] speak, and they followed Jesus. Then Jesus turned, and seeing them following, said to them, "What do you seek?"

They said to Him, "Teacher, where are You staying?"

He said to them, "Come and see."

John 1:37–39

Life is a mysterious journey; we don't always know exactly what we're looking for. Within our hearts we search and do not find; yet there comes a moment when, looking up, we see him. He beckons. We can ignore his gentle invitation and carry on our journey alone, or we can heed his call, come and see him, come and receive what he offers.

A. M.

Him therefore we accompany; him we follow; him have we for guide of our journey; source of light; author of salvation, who promises heaven and the Father to them that believe.

Cyprian of Carthage

You will guide me with Your counsel.

Psalm 73:24

If you would have God hear you when you pray, you must hear him when he speaks.

Thomas Brooks

He that takes truth for his guide, and duty for his end, may safely trust to God's providence to lead him aright.

Blaise Pascal

O Lord, may I be directed what to do and what to leave undone.

Elizabeth Fry

We are silent at the beginning of the day because God should have the first word, and we are silent before going to sleep because the last word also belongs to God.

Dietrich Bonhoeffer

O Lord, to be turned from you is to fall, to turn to you is to rise, and to stand in your presence is to live for ever. Grant us in all our duties your help, in all our perplexities your guidance, in all our dangers your protection, and in all our sorrows your peace; through Jesus Christ our Lord.

Augustine of Hippo

Children are a blessing and a gift from the Lord.

Psalm 127:3 (CEV)

They brought little children to Him, that He might touch them; but the disciples rebuked those who brought them. But when Jesus saw it, He was greatly displeased and said to them,

"Let the little children come to Me, and do not forbid them; for of such is the kingdom of God. Assuredly, I say to you, whoever does not receive the kingdom of God as a little child will by no means enter it."

And He took them up in His arms, put His hands on them, and blessed them.

Mark 10:13–16

When the voices of children
   are heard on the green
And laughing is heard on the hill,
My heart is at rest within my breast
And everything else is still.

William Blake

Jesus answered,
"You say rightly that I am a king."

John 18:37

Rejoice, the Lord is King!
Your Lord and King adore;
Mortals give thanks and sing,
    and triumph evermore;
Lift up your heart, lift up your voice;
Rejoice, again I say, rejoice!
Jesus, the Saviour, reigns,
    the God of truth and love;
When He had purged our stains
He took His seat above;
Lift up your heart, lift up your voice;
    Rejoice, again I say, rejoice!
His kingdom cannot fail,
He rules o'er earth and heav'n,
The keys of death and hell
    are to our Jesus giv'n;
Lift up your heart, lift up your voice;
Rejoice, again I say, rejoice!

Charles Wesley

Blessed is the King who comes in the name of
the LORD! Peace in heaven and glory in the
highest!

Luke 19:38

What does the LORD require of you but to do justly, to love mercy, and to walk humbly with your God?

Micah 6:8 NKJ

Uphold my steps in Your paths,
That my footsteps may not slip.
I have called upon You,
   for You will hear me, O God;
Incline Your ear to me,
   and hear my speech.
Show Your marvelous lovingkindness
   by Your right hand,
O You who save those who trust in You
From those who rise up against them.
Keep me as the apple of Your eye;
Hide me under the shadow of Your wings.

Psalm 17:5–8

O Lord our God, who has called us to serve you
in the midst of the world's affairs,
When we stumble, hold us;
   when we fall, lift us up.
When we are hard pressed with evil,
   deliver us.
When we turn from what is good,
   turn us back
      and bring us at last to your glory.

Alcuin

He is your praise, and He is your God, who has done for you these great and awesome things which your eyes have seen.

Deuteronomy 10:21

Giving God praise is a vital element in our prayers, as Merlin Carothers describes: "Any form of sincere prayer opens the door for God's power to move into our lives, but the prayer of praise releases more of God's power than any other form of petition."

A. M.

Gratitude is not only the memory but the homage of the heart—rendered to God for his goodness.

Nathaniel Parker Willis

Cultivate a thankful spirit! It will be to thee a perpetual feast. There is, or ought to be, with us no such thing as small mercies; all are great, because the least are undeserved. Indeed a really thankful heart will extract motive for gratitude from everything, making the most even of scanty blessings.

John Ross Macduff

Blessed is the nation whose God is the Lord, the people He has chosen as His own inheritance.

Psalm 33:12

Man is never nearer the Divine than in his compassionate moments.

Joseph H. Hertz

[*Hannah*] was in bitterness of soul, and prayed to the LORD and wept in anguish [*because she was childless*]. Now Hannah spoke in her heart; only her lips moved, but her voice was not heard. Therefore Eli [*the priest*] thought she was drunk.

And Hannah answered and said, "No, my lord, I am a woman of sorrowful spirit. I have drunk neither wine nor intoxicating drink, but have poured out my soul before the LORD."

Then Eli answered and said, "Go in peace, and the God of Israel grant your petition which you have asked of Him."

So the woman went her way and ate, and her face was no longer sad.

1 Samuel 1:10–18

When Hannah had prayed, she had peace; she was no more troubled. The soul tossed with a tempest prays, and puts into the will of God, as to a harbour. Here she lies sheltered from every storm. The spirit that rides by prayer into the haven of God's will is fenced from violent blasts by the power and wisdom of God, as high and protective rocks on each side.

Peter Sterry, adapted

An offering ... a sweet aroma to the LORD.

Leviticus 1:9

In the morning, prayer is the key that opens to us the treasure of God's mercies and blessings; in the evening, it is the key that shuts us up under his protection and safeguard. Prayer, as the first, second and third element of the Christian life, should open, prolong and conclude each day.

The first act of the soul in early morning should be a draught at the heavenly fountain. It will sweeten the taste for the day. A few moments with God at that calm and tranquil season, are of more value than much fine gold. And if you tarry long so sweetly at the throne, you will come out of the closet ... suffused all over with the heavenly fragrance of that communion.

Henry Ward Beecher

It is good to give thanks to the LORD,
And to sing praises to Your name,
O Most High;
To declare Your lovingkindness
        in the morning.

Psalm 92:1–2

Exhort one another daily, while it is called "Today."

Hebrews 3:13

As long as it is day, we must do the works of him who sent me. Night is coming, when no one can work.

John 9:4

You have a disagreeable duty to do at twelve o'clock. Do not blacken nine, and ten, and eleven, and all between, with the colour of twelve. Do the work of each, and reap your reward in peace. So when the dreaded moment in the future becomes the present, you shall meet it walking in the light, and that light will overcome its darkness.

George Macdonald

The surest method of arriving at a knowledge of God's eternal purposes about us is to be found in the right use of the present moment. God's will does not come to us in the whole, but in fragments, and generally in small fragments. It is our business to piece it together, and to live it into one orderly vocation.

Frederick W. Faber

**My soul, wait silently for God alone,
for my expectation is from Him.**

Psalm 62:5

Let this season be an advent of a heart of hope. In the words of Reverend Tom Cuthell: "Each year we retell the astonishing entrance that God made into our broken world and we are moved...by God's capacity to surprise us with love. ... The birth of Jesus is God's heartfelt protest against letting things be, abandoning people to their own devices, leaving people to fall back on the threadbare poverty of their own resources. Jesus is the saving, dynamic help of God among us; he is the one Word on God's telegram of hope."

A. M.

O come, Thou Day-spring, come and cheer
Our spirits by Thine advent here.
O come, Desire of nations, bind
In one the hearts of all mankind;
Bid Thou our sad divisions cease,
And be Thyself our King of Peace.

12th century antiphon, translated by John M. Neale

May your unfailing love be with us, Lord, even as we put our hope in you.

Psalm 33:22

I am the Alpha and the Omega, the Beginning and the End.

Revelation 1:8

I have not spoken in secret, in a dark place of the earth; I did not say ... 'Seek Me in vain'; I, the Lord, speak righteousness, I declare things that are right. I'm God, and I act in loyal love. I do what's right and set things right and fair, and delight in those who do the same things. These are my trademarks.

I, the Lord, love justice; I hate robbery. ... Tell the truth, the whole truth, when you speak. Do the right thing by one another, both personally and in your courts. Let none of you think evil in your heart against your neighbor; and do not love a false oath. For all these are things that I hate.

There is no other God but me, a righteous God and Savior. ... Most assuredly, I say to you, he who hears My word and believes in Him who sent Me has everlasting life, and shall not come into judgment, but has passed from death into life.

Isaiah 45:19, Jeremiah 9:24 MSG, Isaiah 61:8, Zechariah 8:16–17 MSG, Isaiah 45:21 NLT, John 5:24

Prophecy never came by the will of man, but holy men of God spoke as they were moved by the Holy Spirit.

2 Peter 1:21

This book [the Bible] had to be written by one of three people: good men, bad men, or God. It couldn't have been written by good men because they said it was inspired by the revelation of God. Good men don't lie and deceive. It couldn't have been written by bad men because bad men would not write something that would condemn themselves. It leaves only one conclusion. It was given by divine inspiration of God.

John Wesley

For this reason we also thank God without ceasing, because when you received the word of God which you heard from us, you welcomed it not as the word of men, but as it is in truth, the word of God, which also effectively works in you who believe.

1 Thessalonians 2:13

The excellent name

O LORD, our Lord,
How excellent is Your name in all the earth,
Who have set Your glory
   above the heavens!
I consider Your heavens,
the work of Your fingers,
The moon and the stars,
which You have ordained.

Psalm 8:1,3

We see as fine risings of the sun as ever Adam saw; and its risings are as much a miracle now as they were in his day—and, I think, a good deal more, because it is now a part of the miracle, that for thousands and thousands of years he has come to his appointed time, without the variation of a millionth part of a second.

Daniel Webster

Taking time to observe the sky above
Reminds us of our Father's love;
He shines his light upon our way,
In night time just as well as day.

A. M.

I press toward the goal for the prize of the upward call of God in Christ Jesus.

Philippians 3:14

The wheels of nature are not made to roll backward; everything presses on towards eternity; from the birth of time an impetuous current has set in, which bears all the sons of man to that interminable ocean.

Robert Hall

Light tomorrow with today!

Elizabeth Barrett Browning

Yesterday is gone. Tomorrow has not yet come. We have only today. Let us begin.

Mother Teresa

Lord,
when you call us to live and work for you,
give us the wisdom to remember
that it is not the beginning
but the faithful continuing of the task
that is most important in your eyes,
until we have completed it
to the best of our ability;
through Jesus Christ, our Lord,
who laid down his life for us
in order to finish your work.

Sir Francis Drake

See, I have inscribed you on the palms of My hands.

Isaiah 49:16

What matters supremely...is not...the fact that I know God, but the larger fact which underlies it—that *he knows me*. I am graven on the palms of his hands. I am never out of his mind. ... He knows me as a friend, one who loves me; and there is no moment when his eye is off me, or his attention distracted from me, and no moment, therefore, when his care falters.

J. I. Packer

As small as we each may feel, as insignificant as we judge ourselves to be in the great scope of the world and history, God thinks about us. The God who set the great creation into motion, the same God knows the very hairs of our head.[1] He knows our thoughts and plans.[2] He knows our secret sorrows just as He knows our wishes: "Lord, all my desire is before You; And my sighing is not hidden from You."[3]

We are not alone in the universe; God knows and loves us.[4]

A. M. [1] Luke 12:7 [2] Hebrews 4:12 [3] Psalm 38:9 [4] John 3:16

We walk by faith, not by sight.

2 Corinthians 5:7

By faith Abraham obeyed when he was called to go out to the place which he would receive as an inheritance. And he went out, not knowing where he was going. By faith he dwelt in the land of promise as in a foreign country, dwelling in tents with Isaac and Jacob, the heirs with him of the same promise; for he waited for the city which has foundations, whose builder and maker is God.

Hebrews 11:8–10

Faith must go before, and then feeling will follow. Though you feel not as you would, yet doubt not, but hope beyond all hope, as Abraham did; for always, faith goes before feeling.

John Bradford

Like legs, faith and works should travel side-by-side, step answering to step, like the legs of men walking. First faith, and then works; and then faith again, and then works again—until they can scarcely distinguish which is the one and which is the other.

William Booth

What a comfort to know that we have a great Physician who is both able and willing to heal us!

Charles Haddon Spurgeon

They brought to Him one who was deaf and had an impediment in his speech, and they begged Him to put His hand on him.

And He took him aside from the multitude, and put His fingers in his ears, and He spat and touched his tongue. Then, looking up to heaven, He sighed, and said to him, "Ephphatha," that is, "Be opened."

Immediately his ears were opened, and the impediment of his tongue was loosed, and he spoke plainly. And [the people] were astonished beyond measure, saying, "He has done all things well. He makes both the deaf to hear and the mute to speak."

Mark 7:32–35,37

There is healing in the Promise,
There is healing in the Blood,
There is strength for all our weakness
In the Risen Son of God.
And the feeblest of His children
All His glorious life may share,
He has better balm in Gilead;
He's the Great Physician there.

Albert Benjamin Simpson

Yet will I rejoice

Though the fig tree may not blossom,
Nor fruit be on the vines;
Though the labor of the olive may fail,
And the fields yield no food;
Though the flock
may be cut off from the fold,
And there be no herd in the stalls—
Yet I will rejoice in the LORD,
I will joy in the God of my salvation.

Habakkuk 3:17–18

Jonah was the man who ran away from God and ended up in the belly of a whale or great fish.[1] This part of the Bible story is well known, along with his subsequent escape and arrival in Nineveh, but we must turn our attention to Jonah while he was *inside* the fish's belly in order to grasp one of the key lessons: Jonah was not delivered as soon as he prayed. It took more than pleading with God to escape from this hell. It required *praise*. It was only when he declared, "I'll call out in thanksgiving!" that the God of salvation brought him out.[2] Praising God in the midst of trouble is the surest route to deliverance.

A. M. [1]Jonah 2; [2]Jonah 2:9–10

How sweet is his smile
in whose countenance heaven lies.

Robert Fleming

Nicholas of Myra, in present-day Turkey, was born in the fourth century to wealthy parents who died when he was a child. As a young man, Nicholas dedicated his life to God, obeyed Jesus' admonition to "sell what you have and give to the poor,"[1] and used his inheritance to assist the needy and the suffering. He was eventually promoted to the office of bishop, and became known for his love and generosity.

His story is a reminder that love means going out of our way to help others; helping others in practical ways and showing kindness are our responsibilities to those we pass by on the road of life.

[1]*Matthew 19:21*

During a long life I have proved that not one kind word ever spoken, not one kind deed ever done, but sooner or later returns to bless the giver, and becomes a chain binding men with golden bands to the throne of God.

Lord Shaftesbury

Nothing too little

Nothing is too little to be ordered by our Father; nothing too little in which to see His hand; nothing which touches our souls too little to accept from Him; nothing too little to be done to Him.

Edward Pusey

God is infinitely patient. He waits for the perfect ripening of things; he waits for the coming of things in their own proper time and order. He has ever an unbroken eternity to work in, and, therefore, he has not the need for haste that the shortness and uncertainty of our life seems to urge upon us at all time. He waits to be gracious.

Hugh Macmillan, adapted

I will remember the works of the LORD;
Surely I will remember Your wonders of old.
I will also meditate on all Your work,
And talk of Your deeds.
You are the God who does wonders;
You have declared Your strength
   among the peoples.
You have with Your arm
redeemed Your people.
When I remember these things,
I pour out my soul in me.
My heart rejoices in the LORD.

Psalm 77:11–15; 42:4; 1 Samuel 2:1

**Seek the LORD while He may be found,
Call upon Him while He is near.**

Isaiah 55:6

Two men please God—who serves him with all his heart because he knows him, who seeks him with all his heart because he knows him not.

Nikita Ivanovich Panin

Eternal Trinity, you are a deep sea,
    into which the more I enter the more I find,
        and the more I find the more I seek.
The soul ever hungers in your abyss,
    Eternal Trinity,
longing to see you with the light of your light,
    and as the deer yearns
        for the springs of water,
so my soul yearns to see you in truth.

Catherine of Siena

If you seek Christ, carry nothing with you. All you need in life, in death, and for eternity, is to be found in him.

William Howells

Set your mind on things above, not on things on the earth.

Colossians 3:2

The world is but a great inn, where we are to stay a night or two, and be gone; what madness is it so to set our heart upon our inn, as to forget our home?

Thomas Watson

The only way to get our values right is to see, not the beginning, but the end of the way, to see things, not in the light of time, but in the light of eternity.

William Barclay

Leave behind what is simply good in exchange for the eternal.

Spanish proverb

The love of heaven makes one heavenly.

William Shakespeare

Do not labor for the food which perishes, but for the food which endures to everlasting life, which the Son of Man will give you, because God the Father has set His seal on Him.

John 6:27

Let the hearts of those rejoice who seek the LORD!

1 Chronicles 16:10

God is great, and therefore he will be sought; he is good, and therefore he will be found.

John Jay

Blessed Saviour, let me find you,
Keep me close to you,
Cast me not behind you.
Life of life, my heart you still
Calm I rest upon your breast
All the void you fill.

Paul Gerhardt

None but God can satisfy the longing of the immortal soul; as the heart was made for him, he only can fill it.

Richard Chenevix Trench

How can you expect God to speak in that gentle and inward voice which melts the soul, when you are making so much noise with your rapid reflections? Be silent, and God will speak again.

François de la Mothe-Fénelon

I will meditate on Your precepts,
And contemplate Your ways.

Psalm 119:15

Enoch walked with God.

Genesis 5:22

ALAS, my God, that we should be
Such strangers to each other!
O that as friends we might agree,
And walk and talk together!
May I taste that communion, Lord,
Thy people have with Thee?
Thy Spirit daily talks with them,
O let It talk with me!

Like Enoch, let me walk with God,
And thus walk out my day,
Attended with the heavenly Guards,
Upon the King's highway.
When wilt Thou come unto me, Lord?
O come, my LORD most dear!
Come near, come nearer, nearer still:
I'm well when Thou art near.

Thomas Shepherd

What matters supremely...is not...the fact that I
know God, but the larger fact which underlies
it—that *he knows me*. I am graven on the
palms of his hands. I am never out of his mind.
... He knows me as a friend, one who loves me;
and there is no moment when his eye is off me,
or his attention distracted from me, and no
moment, therefore, when his care falters.

J. I. Packer

Give us this day our daily bread.

Luke 11:3

Bread is the food most frequently mentioned in the Bible. *Lehem*, the Hebrew word for bread in the Old Testament, is used 295 times. In the New Testament, the Greek word is *artos*, and it is used 98 times. The Bible lists breads made of wheat, barley, rye, beans, lentils, millet, and even manna. They would have been cooked on flat stones or iron griddles, perhaps in an oven; they would have been flat and hard, or leavened cakes.

Bread is a metaphor for the sustenance of life, both literal and figurative. We are not to "live by bread alone," but "by every word that proceeds out of the mouth of the Lord."[1]

God nourishes our bodies, our minds, and our spirits. For his provision of our needs—both literal and spiritual—let us say 'thank you'.

A. M. [1] Matthew 4:4, Deuteronomy 8:3

He makes grass grow for the cattle,
and plants for people to cultivate—
bringing forth food from the earth:
wine that gladdens human hearts,
oil to make their faces shine,
and bread that sustains their hearts.

Psalm 104:14–15 NIV

He makes His sun rise.

Matthew 5:45

The LORD bless you and keep you;
The LORD make His face shine upon you,
And be gracious to you;
The LORD lift up His countenance upon you,
And give you peace.

Numbers 6:24–26

We have a Friend and Protector, from whom, if we do not ourselves depart from him, no power nor spirit can separate us. In his strength let us proceed on our journey, through the storms, and troubles, and dangers of the world. However they may rage and swell, though the mountains shake at the tempests, our rock will not be moved:[1] we have one friend who will never forsake us;[2] one refuge, where we may rest in peace and stand in our lot at the end of the days.[3]

Reginald Heber. [1] *Psalm 46:2;* [2] *Hebrews 13:5;* [3] *Psalm 46:1; Daniel 12:13*

Turn your eyes upon Jesus,
Look full in His wonderful face,
And the things of earth
will grow strangely dim,
In the light of His glory and grace.

Helen H. Lemmel

Then He arose and rebuked the wind, and said to the sea, "Peace, be still!" And the wind ceased and there was a great calm.

Mark 4:39

Your external circumstances may change, toil may take the place of rest, sickness of health, trials may thicken within and without. Externally, you are the prey of such circumstances; but if your heart is stayed on God, no changes or chances can touch it, and all that may befall you will but draw you closer to Him. ... He who holds you in His powerful hand cannot change, but abideth forever.

Jean Nicolas Grou

Drop Thy still dews of quietness,
Till all our strivings cease:
Take from our souls the strain and stress,
And let our ordered lives confess
The beauty of Thy peace.

Breathe through the heats of our desire
Thy coolness and Thy balm;
Let sense be dumb, let flesh retire;
Speak through the earthquake,
    wind and fire,
O still small voice of calm!

John Greenleaf Whittier

You are my hiding place;
You shall preserve me from trouble;
You shall surround me with songs of
deliverance.

Psalm 32:7

The Lord is always a sanctuary or hiding place to his children; in every place, in every company, they may hide in the secret of his presence from the strife of tongues about them. Better never enter into society, even into that of Christians, than go without taking our hiding place within us.

Mary Anne Schimmelpenninck

I put aside my weighty cares and leave my wearisome toils for a while. I abandon myself to you, O God, and rest for a little in you.

I enter the inner chamber of my soul, and seek only God and the things that can help me in my quest for you.

Come then, Lord my God, teach my heart where and how to look for you, where and how to find you.

Anselm of Canterbury

Blessed [are] the meek,
For they shall inherit the earth.

Matthew 5:5

The meek man will attain a place of soul rest. As he walks on in meekness he will be happy to let God defend him. The old struggle to defend himself is over. He has found the peace which meekness brings.

Aiden Wilson Tozer

The meek have a special place in the Lord's heart and He makes special promises to them.

Author unknown

The meek shall eat and be satisfied. For the Lord takes pleasure in His people: He will beautify the meek with salvation.

Psalm 22:26, 149:4, adapted

Lord, teach me the silence of love, the silence of wisdom, the silence of humility, the silence of faith, the silence that speaks without words.

O Saviour, teach me to silence my heart that I may listen to the gentle movement of the Holy Spirit within me, and sense the depths that are God, today and always.

Frankfurt, sixteenth century

**Do not worry about tomorrow,
for tomorrow will worry
about its own things.
Sufficient for the day is its own trouble.**

Matthew 6:34

Lord, while we wait the moment

When we shall see Thy face,
We daily prove the sweetness
Of Thy sustaining grace;
Yea, daily find the comfort
Of Thine unfailing love,
Till we shall know its fulness
When with Thee, Lord, above.

And yet while in the desert,
What lessons do we learn,
As on our homeward journey
Thou mak'st our hearts to burn!
The living water flowing
From life's perennial spring,
The daily manna coming,
Fresh praises daily bring.

Frances George Burkitt

Look upon every day as the whole of life, not
merely as a section; and enjoy and improve the
present without wishing, through haste, to rush
on to another.

Jean Paul Richter

We must accept finite disappointment, but we must never lose infinite hope.

Martin Luther King, Jr.

Cold winds have whipped through the trees, stripping them of their autumn foliage. Bare branches stand silhouetted against the grey sky; the outlook is bleak. But although "weeping may last all night ... joy comes in the morning."[1] Despite outward appearances, life still remains in the heart of the tree; in the morning of springtime the sap will flow up through the branches, leaves will grow again. Even so, on occasions of disappointment when all seems lost, keep hope; in time, good things will come again.

A. M. [1]*Psalm 30:5*

My life is like a faded leaf,
My harvest dwindled to a husk:
Truly my life is void and brief
And tedious in the barren dusk:
My life is like a frozen thing,
No bud nor greenness can I see,
Yet rise it shall — the sap of spring,
O Jesus, rise in me.

Christina Rossetti

I lie awake, and am like a sparrow alone on the housetop.

Psalm 102:7

My soul longs, yes, even faints
For the courts of the LORD;
My heart and my flesh cry out for the living God.

Psalm 84:2

Calm my troubled heart; give me peace.

O Lord, calm the waves of this heart, calm its tempests!

Calm thyself, O my soul, so that the divine can act in thee!

Calm thyself, O my soul, so that God is able to repose in thee, so that His peace may cover thee!

Yes, Father in heaven, often have we found that the world cannot give us peace, but make us feel that thou art able to give peace; let us know the truth of thy promise: that the whole world may not be able to take away thy peace.

Søren Kierkegaard

Peace be with you; do not fear.

Judges 6:23

If you fear, cast all your fear on God; that anchor holds.

Lord Alfred Tennyson

The fact that the early Christians often used the symbol of the fish to signal their faith to fellow-believers is common knowledge; their use of an anchor is less well known. From ancient times, the anchor was viewed as a symbol of safety. For Christians, the anchor symbolised their hope in Christ, who would bring them to the safe harbour of his heavenly kingdom. Anchors adorn numerous tombs of early Christians buried in the catacombs beneath Rome.

We have hope in Christ; we can rest secure in the knowledge that he will hold us steady in the storms of life.

A. M.

These things I have spoken to you, that in Me you may have peace. In the world you will have tribulation; but be of good cheer, I have overcome the world.

John 16:33

**Out of the depths I have cried to You,
O LORD; Lord, hear my voice!**

Psalm 130:1–2

God is our refuge and strength,
A very present help in trouble.
Therefore we will not fear,
Even though the earth be removed,
And though the mountains be carried into the
midst of the sea;
Though its waters roar and be troubled,
Though the mountains shake with its swelling.

Psalm 46:1–3

O Lord, support us all the day long of this
troublous life, until the shadows lengthen and
the evening comes, and the busy world is
hushed, and the fever of life is over and our
work is done. Then, Lord, in thy mercy, grant
us a safe lodging, a holy rest, and peace at the
last.

Attributed to John Henry Newman

Nature is the living, visible garment of God.

Johann Wolfgang von Goethe

Like valleys that stretch out,
Like gardens by the riverside,
Like aloes planted by the LORD,
Like cedars beside the waters.

Numbers 24:6

Surely there is something in the unruffled calm of nature that overawes our little anxieties and doubts: the sight of the deep-blue sky, and the clustering stars above, seem to impart a quiet to the mind.

Jonathan Edwards

Earth with her thousand voices praises God.

Samuel Taylor Coleridge

Nature is man's teacher. She unfolds her treasures to his search, unseals his eye, illumes his mind, and purifies his heart; an influence breathes from all the sights and sounds of her existence.

Alfred Billings Street

Anyone who keeps the ability to see beauty never grows old.

Franz Kafka

Stand still and consider the wondrous works of God.

Job 37:14

See how the farmer waits for the precious fruit of the earth, waiting patiently for it until it receives the early and latter rain.

James 5:7

God is teaching you by His great picture book of nature to wait, to sow your seed, and wait for the slow ripening of the harvest under the patient heavens. He does not give you perfect and full-formed things at once. He sows the seeds of things that will gradually grow and ripen and bear fruit. He gives buds first, and then full unfolded blossoms, and then perfect fruit. "Everything comes to him that has patience to wait for it" is a proverb the truth of which has often been proved.

Let your apple blossoms remain ungathered on the tree, and they will grow into apples in their own good time.

Hugh Macmillan, adapted

Though today may not fulfil
All your hopes, have patience still;
For perchance tomorrow's sun
Sees your happier days begun.

Author unknown

**Let us adore Him,
and praise His great love;
To save us poor sinners
He came from above.**

Henry Ramsden Bramley

Joseph went up [to] Bethlehem, to be registered with Mary, his betrothed wife, who was with child. So it was, that while they were there, the days were completed for her to be delivered. And she brought forth her firstborn Son, and wrapped Him in swaddling cloths, and laid Him in a manger, because there was no room for them in the inn.

Now there were in the same country shepherds living out in the fields, keeping watch over their flock by night. And behold, an angel of the Lord stood before them [and] said, "Do not be afraid, for behold, I bring you good tidings of great joy which will be to all people. For there is born to you this day in the city of David a Savior, who is Christ the Lord. And this will be the sign to you: You will find a Babe wrapped in swaddling cloths, lying in a manger."

And suddenly there was with the angel a multitude of the heavenly host praising God and saying: "Glory to God in the highest, And on earth peace, goodwill toward men!" So it was, that the shepherds came with haste and found Mary and Joseph, and the Babe lying in a manger.

Luke 2:1–16, abridged

Christmas Day

Loving God, help us to remember the birth of Jesus that we may share in the songs of the angels, the gladness of the shepherds, and the worship of the wise men. Close the door of hate and open the door of love all over the world. Let kindness come with every gift and good desires with every greeting. Deliver us from evil by the blessing which Christ brings. May our minds be filled with grateful thoughts and our hearts with forgiveness, for Jesus' sake. Amen.

Robert Louis Stevenson

O holy Child of Bethlehem,
    descend to us, we pray;
Cast out our sin, and enter in,
    be born in us today.
We hear the Christmas angels
    the great glad tidings tell;
O come to us, abide with us,
    our Lord Emmanuel!

Phillip Brooks

What is Christmas?

What is Christmas? It is tenderness for the past, courage for the present, hope for the future. It is a fervent wish that every cup may overflow with blessings rich and eternal, and that every path may lead to peace.

Agnes M. Pharo

There is a lot going on this Christmas. But it is not in the shops and the parties and the pulsating lights. To be part of it you need to find time to be quiet, to be silent and still, to contemplate his presence in your hearts and in your minds. He is there. He wants to embrace you. Let him.

And having discovered what is really going on at Christmas we cannot, in the end, keep quiet about it. We cannot live in a world that, in spite of the tragedies and sorrows, is still a world full of gifts, without saying "thank you." We cannot be part of what Christmas is really about without praising and glorifying God as Mary did. We cannot be fully human unless we let ourselves sing along with her those words of heaven-filled gratitude: "My soul glorifies the Lord. My spirit rejoices in God my Saviour. He who is mighty has done great things for me and holy is his name."[1]

Cormac Murphy-O'Connor. [1]Luke 1:46–47, 49

Dear Jesus, God and man

You left your throne of immortality and encased yourself in human flesh. You became one of us, so that you could save us. Joy floods my heart when I think of how you quietly and humbly came into our world and changed it forever. Who could have imagined the transformation that would come through a little baby, born to commoners, wrapped in rags, sleeping in a feeding trough?

Thank you for making the choice to experience both the joys and sorrows of our earthly life. Thank you for enduring the tears, pain, frustration, loneliness, exhaustion and finally death so that you could truly understand us. Never has there been a more perfect love than yours!

Please forgive my mistakes and shortcomings. You are the Saviour of the world—I want you to be my personal Saviour too. I invite you into my heart. Walk beside me all the days of my life, and when my time here draws to its close, please bring me to heaven to live forever with you. Amen.

Grow in grace.

2 Peter 3:18

Everyone who competes in the games goes into strict training. They do it to get a crown that will not last, but we do it to get a crown that will last forever. Therefore I do not run like someone running aimlessly; I do not fight like a boxer beating the air.

1 Corinthians 9:25–26 NIV

Life is change. Growth is optional. Choose wisely.

Author unknown

Growing spiritually can be like a roller coaster ride. Take comfort in the knowledge that the way down is only preparation for the way up.

Rebbe Nachman

Let us labour to be like unto angels, "strengthened with all might," walking about the world as conquerors, able to do all things through Christ which strengthens us.[1]

John Trapp. [1]Philippians 4:13

But we all, with unveiled face, beholding as in a mirror the glory of the Lord, are being transformed into the same image from glory to glory, just as by the Spirit of the Lord.

2 Corinthians 3:18

Does He not see my ways, and count all my steps?

Job 31:4

Nathanael was living in first century Palestine under the shadow of a brutal military occupation. As he sat alone under a fig tree, perhaps he was reflecting on these circumstances, or perhaps he was in prayer. Later his friend Phillip brought him to meet Jesus.

When Jesus saw Nathanael, he said, "There's a real Israelite, not a false bone in his body." Nathanael replied, "Where did you get that idea? You don't know me." Jesus answered, "One day, long before Philip called you here, I saw you under the fig tree."

Nathanael was astonished to find out that God had been watching him; God knew him. This realization inspired him to proclaim that Jesus was the Son of God.

We are not unknown to God. Even if nobody else seems to be thinking about us, it's quite certain that God is. He's been watching over us in love our entire lives, even before we were born, and all the days since.

Based on John 1:45–49 and Psalm 139:2–3

You need not cry very loud; he is nearer to us than we think.

Brother Lawrence

At the closing of the year

The year is closed, the record made
The last deed done, the last word said,
The memory alone remains
Of all its joys, its grief, its gains
And now with purpose full and clear,
We turn to meet another year.

Robert Browning

Our years come to an end like a sigh.

Psalm 90:9 NRSV

The path of the past year is ending; the path of a new year is about to begin. The future is hidden from our sight, as the old proverb tells us, "The veil that hides the future from us is woven by an angel of mercy." That leaves us in the present—this moment. God is here with us in the present, just as He was in the past and will be in the future. Let's finish this year by acknowledging the One who is the beginning and the end.[1]

He is with us always: at the start, at the finish, and all the way through.

A. M. [1] *Revelation 22:13*

Here we have no continuing city, but we seek the one to come.

Hebrews 13:14

There is One amid all changes
Who standeth ever fast,
One who covers all the future,
The present and the past;
Jesus is the first,
Jesus is the last,
Trust Him for thy future,
Leave with Him the past;
Christ the Rock of Ages,
The first and the last.

Albert Benjamin Simpson

Jesus is "the Alpha and the Omega, the Beginning and the End, the First and the Last."[1] He is "the same, yesterday, today, and forever."[2] And he assures us he is with us always.[3] On such a foundation we can stake our future with confidence.

[1]Revelation 22:13; [2]Hebrews 13:8; [3]Matthew 28:20

O Lord, as the years change, may we find rest in your eternal changelessness. Help us to meet this coming year bravely, in the faith that, while life changes all around us, you are always the same, guiding us with your wisdom and protecting us with your love; through our Saviour Jesus Christ.

William Temple, adapted

APPENDIX

THE CHRISTIAN CALENDAR

This is a guide to where to find readings
for principle events on the Christian calendar.
(The dates of some of these are consistent,
but others differ year by year
and/or by denomination.)

Epiphany: January 6
Palm Sunday: April 6
Good Friday: April 11
Easter Sunday: Easter (back of book)
Ascension: June 2
Pentecost: Pentecost (back of book)
All Saints' Day: November 1
First Sunday of Advent: November 27
Christmas Eve: December 24
Christmas Day: December 25

[Jesus] was buried,
and He rose again the third day.

1 Corinthians 15:4

Lift your voices in triumph on high
For Jesus is risen and man cannot die.

Henry Ware

The simple message that changed the world forever was this one: "He is not here. He is risen."

Linda Bowles

Jesus departed from our sight that we might return to our heart and there find him. For he departed and, behold, he is here.

Augustine of Hippo

Easter means hope prevails over despair. Jesus reigns as Lord of lords and King of kings. ... Easter says to us that despite everything to the contrary, His will for us will prevail, love will prevail over hate, justice over injustice and oppression, peace over exploitation and bitterness.

Desmond Tutu

Jesus said to her, "I am the resurrection and the life. He who believes in Me, though he may die, he shall live. And whoever lives and believes in Me shall never die."

John 11:25–26

Pentecost

When the Day of Pentecost had fully come, they were all with one accord in one place.

And suddenly there came a sound from heaven, as of a rushing mighty wind, and it filled the whole house where they were sitting. Then there appeared to them divided tongues, as of fire, and one sat upon each of them. And they were all filled with the Holy Spirit and began to speak with other tongues, as the Spirit gave them utterance.

And when this sound occurred, the multitude came together, and were confused, because everyone heard them speak in his own language. Then they were all amazed and marveled, saying to one another,

"Look, are not all these who speak Galileans? And how is it that we hear, each in our own language in which we were born?—We hear them speaking in our own tongues the wonderful works of God."

Then those who gladly received his word were baptized; and that day about three thousand souls were added to them.

Acts 2:1–4, 6–11, 41

SUBJECT INDEX

#0154 - 190916 - C0 - 175/108/20 - PB - DID1588121